The Hurried Child

DAVID ELKIND

The Hurried Child

Growing Up Too Fast Too Soon

ADDISON-WESLEY PUBLISHING COMPANY

Reading, Massachusetts • Menlo Park, California • London

Amsterdam • Don Mills, Ontario • Sydney

Library of Congress Cataloging in Publication Data

Elkind, David, 1931–
  The hurried child.

  Includes index.
  1. Child mental health. 2. Stress (Psychology)
I. Title
RJ499.E415   305.2'3   81-14842
ISBN 0-201-03966-4   AACR2
ISBN 0-201-03967-2 (pbk.)

Permission has been granted to use "(Let Me Be) Your Teddy Bear" by Kal Mann and Bernie Lowe, © 1957 by Gladys Music. All rights controlled by Chappell & Co., Inc. (Intersong Music Publisher). International copyright secured. All rights reserved.

Permission has been granted to use "Diana," © 1957. Words and music by Paul Anka. Spanka Music Corp. Published by Management Agency & Music Publishing, Inc. All rights reserved.

ISBN 0-201-03967-2 (pb.)
ISBN 0-201-03966-4
J-DO-89876543

Tenth Printing, September 1983

Cover by Marshall Henrichs

To Ruth, with love and appreciation

Acknowledgments

Many different people contributed in many different ways to the writing of this book. Friends like Nina Compton de Willock, Nancy Rambusch, Otto and Sylvia Weininger, and Miriam Costello offered support and encouragement, as well as relevant clippings and articles. Dr. Jane Prager gave me valuable feedback on some of the dynamic formulations I presented and helped allay some of my fears about writing a "popular" book. My sons, Paul, Robert, and Rick, were patient with my retreats into the study and were generous with examples and open to discussing book-related issues. I am especially indebted to my departmental assistant, Louise Clancy, who typed the manuscript with speed and good humor despite my hurried writing and bad spelling. Last of all, I owe many thanks to Dorothy Coover, my guardian angel at Addison Wesley. Doe put a great deal of time and energy into the book and shepherded it from start to completion. Her warmth and consideration were a special bonus.

South Yarmouth, Massachusetts
20 August 1981

Contents

Prologue

Over a year ago I was interviewed by a reporter who was doing an article on the spoiled child. While I hadn't thought about it much before, I realized that as a child professional who sees all kinds of troubled children, I rarely see today what once was so common—namely, spoiled children. Most of the middle-class spoiled children were shaped by attitudes and child-rearing practices quite different from what is common among contemporary parents.

In the 1940s and 1950s, the Freudian influence was great and many middle-class parents were afraid of repressing their children and of making them neurotic through too much discipline. This was of course a misreading of Freud (who was in favor of discipline), but the attitude was widespread and went beyond the home. I used to dread visiting a nursery school run on this philosophy because I was inevitably pelted with clay or splashed with paint while teachers looked on with beatific smiles, happy that the children were "expressing themselves." Such children, left largely undisciplined and unconstrained by demands to grow up, indulged their most primitive impulses. But children need and want help in controlling their impulses; if they are not called upon to control themselves, they use their behavior to control adults. Yet in fact it is scary to a child to have power over adults. Consequently, handed a power they did not want, did not need, and could not handle, such children were willful, domineering, given to temper tantrums, and on the whole abominable.

The reporter's question thus brought to consciousness a phenomenon that I had been seeing and writing about for more than a decade but had never really pinpointed before. To illustrate, since the late 1960s I have written often about the dangers of introducing formal instruction in reading before children have the requisite mental abilities. And I have also written about "curriculum-disabled" children who became "disabled" by unteachable and unlearnable curriculum materials. What I realized was that I and other child professionals were no longer dealing with spoiled children. Rather, these children seemed to have too much pressure to achieve, to succeed, to please. It was not the lack of pressure of earlier generations, but a new pressure to hurry and grow up. Unlike the spoiled children who remain children too long, hurried children grow up too fast, pushed in their early years toward many different types of achievement and exposed to experiences that tax their adaptive capacity. Just as, at bottom, spoiled children were stressed by the fear of their own power, hurried children are stressed by the fear of failure—of not achieving fast enough or high enough.

Hurried children are forced to take on the physical, psychological, and social trappings of adulthood before they are prepared to deal with them. We dress our children in miniature adult costumes (often with designer labels), we expose them to gratuitous sex and violence, and we expect them to cope with an increasingly bewildering social environment—divorce, single parenthood, homosexuality. Through all of these pressures the child senses that it is important for him or her to cope without admitting the confusion and pain that accompany such changes. Like adults, they are made to feel they must be survivors, and surviving means adjusting—even if the survivor is only four or six or eight years old. This pressure to cope without cracking is a stress in itself, the effects of which must be tallied with all the other effects of hurrying our children.

Hurried children seem to make up a large portion of the troubled children seen by clinicians today; they constitute many of the young people experiencing school failure, those involved in delinquency and drugs, and those who are committing suicide. They also include many of the children who have chronic psychosomatic complaints such as headaches and stomachaches, who are chronically unhappy, hyperactive, or lethargic and unmotivated. These diseases and problems have long been recognized as stress related in adults, and it is time we looked at children and stress in the same light. Yet the syndrome has not been well described in the professional literature, nor is it well known in a systematic way by parents. Hence this book is meant to bring together our knowledge about stress and hurried children, how and why they became the way they are and also how we can identify and help them.

Part I

Our Hurried Children

Chapter 1

Our Hurried Children

*T*he concept of childhood, so vital to the traditional American way of life, is threatened with extinction in the society we have created. Today's child has become the unwilling, unintended victim of overwhelming stress—the stress borne of rapid, bewildering social change and constantly rising expectations. The contemporary parent dwells in a pressure-cooker of competing demands, transitions, role changes, personal and professional uncertainties, over which he or she exerts slight direction. We seek release from stress whenever we can, and usually the one sure ambit of our control is the home. Here, if nowhere else, we enjoy the fact (or illusion) of playing a determining role. If child-rearing necessarily entails stress, then by hurrying children to grow up, or by treating them as adults, we hope to remove a portion of our burden of worry and anxiety and to enlist our children's aid in carrying life's load. We do not mean our children harm in acting thus—on the contrary, as a society we have come to imagine that it is good for young people to mature rapidly. Yet we do our children harm when we hurry them through childhood.

The principal architect of our modern notion of childhood was the French philosopher Jean-Jacques Rousseau. It was he who first criticized the educational methods for presenting materials from a uniquely adult perspective, reflecting adult values and interests. Classical *paideia*—that is, the value of transmitting a cultural-social heritage—was a good thing, said Rousseau, but the learning process must take the child's perceptions and stage of development into account. In his classic work *Emile*, Rousseau wrote, "Childhood has its own way of seeing, thinking, and feeling, and nothing is more foolish than to try to substitute ours for theirs." More specifically, he observed that children matured in four stages, and just as each stage had its own characteristics, it should also have a corresponding set of appropriate educational objectives.[1]

This idea of childhood as a distinct phase preceding adult life became inextricably interwoven with the modern concepts of universal education and the small, nuclear family (mother, father, children—not the extended family of earlier eras) in the late eighteenth and early nineteenth centuries, the heyday of the original Industrial Revolution. The transition is well explained by futurologist Alvin Toffler: "As work shifted out of the fields and the home, children had to be prepared for factory life. . . . If young people could be pre-fitted in the industrial system, it would vastly ease the problems of industrial discipline later on. The result was another central structure of all [modern] societies: mass education."[2]

In addition to free, universal, public education, the emergent society tended to create smaller family units. Toffler writes, "To free workers for factory labor, key functions of the family were parcelled out to new specialized institutions. Education of the child was turned over to schools. Care of the aged was turned over to the poor houses or old-age homes or nursing homes. Above all, the new society required mobility. It needed workers who would follow jobs from place to place. . . . Torn apart by migration to the cities, battered by economic storms, families stripped themselves of unwanted relatives, grew smaller, more mobile, more suited to the needs of the [work place]."[3]

While industrialization proceeded apace, the cultural recognition of childhood as a discrete life phase was given strong social reinforcement in the late nineteenth century with the establishment of child psychology as a scientific discipline. Work in this field began with the so-called baby biographies—minutely detailed accounts by observant parents of their infants' behavior. Bronson Alcott, father of Louisa May, contributed one such study, as did Milicent Shinn.[4] Jean Piaget, the celebrated Swiss psychologist, carried on the tradition when he took time off from his collective studies of children to observe at close range (and write about) his own three offspring.[5]

Around the turn of the century, G. Stanley Hall, generally regarded as the founder of the laboratory study of children, initiated
the ill-fated "Child Study Movement." The extensive questionnaires
he designed that parents and teachers administered to children by
the thousands proved to be terribly error-prone and inexact. However, Hall had more success in founding Clark University, and the
school's department of child psychology, carefully cultivated by
Hall, led the nation in research and training in the new field, producing scientists of the eminence of Arnold Gessell and Lewis
Terman.

After the Second World War, child psychology entered its boom
period. Whereas before the war there were only two scientific jour-
nals reporting research in child development, today there are more
than a dozen. All university departments of psychology include psychologists who are studying topics as varied as adolescence, learning in infants, socialization, peer interaction, sexual development,
attachment and loss, the measurement of intelligence, learning dis-
abilities, language acquisition, and so on. In short, we have accumulated a large library of data and knowledge about the period of life
we call childhood. It is indeed no small irony that at the very time
the stress of social life and change is threatening the existence of
childhood, we know far more about childhood than we have ever
known in the past.

What is even more curious is the degree to which this scientific
knowledge is available to and consumed by the general public, for
the research explosion in child study has been matched by a corresponding blaze of popular books about children. Often, well-known
child psychologists undertake to "translate" scientific findings into
useful applications. As early as 1894, the renowned psychologist T.
Emmet Holt informed readers of his book *Care and Feeding of Children* how to prevent chafing: "First, not too much or too strong soap
should be used; secondly, careful rinsing of the body, thirdly, not
too vigorous rubbing, either during or after the bath; fourthly, the
very free use of dusting powder in all the folds of the skin. . . . This is
of the utmost importance in very fat infants."[7] Holt was merely the
first in a seemingly endless line of distinguished (and not so distinguished) "translators" of scientific child psychology into a popular idiom. Perhaps the two best-known are Arnold Gesell's *The*

Child from Birth to Five and the incomparably influential *Infant and Child Care* by Dr. Benjamin Spock.[7] Yet each year an awesome number of books, some very well written and others less so, appear with titles like (to consider just 1977) *Raising Happy Healthy Children, For Love of Children, Parenting, The Parent Book, Living with Your Hyperactive Children,* and *Helping Your Child Learn Right from Wrong.*[8] Workshops and courses are available in every community in the country to guide and assist adults involved with the rearing of young people. If we hurry children to grow up too fast today, then, it is surely not done out of ignorance.

MINIATURE ADULTS

Today's pressures on middle-class children to grow up fast begin in early childhood. Chief among them is the pressure for early intellectual attainment, deriving from a changed perception of precocity. Several decades ago precocity was looked upon with great suspicion. The child prodigy, it was thought, turned out to be a neurotic adult; thus the phrase "early ripe, early rot!" Trying to accelerate children's acquisition of academic skills was seen as evidence of bad parenting.

A good example of this type of attitude is provided by the case of William James Sidis, the son of a psychiatrist. Sidis was born at the turn of the century and became a celebrated child prodigy who entered Harvard College at the age of eleven. His papers on higher mathematics gave the impression that he would make major contributions in this area. Sidis soon attracted the attention of the media, who celebrated his feats as a child. But Sidis never went further and seemed to move aimlessly from one job to another. In 1930 James Thurber wrote a profile of Sidis in the *New Yorker* Magazine entitled "Where Are They Now?"; he described Sidis's lonely and pitiful existence in which his major preoccupation was collecting streetcar transfers from all over the world.

Such attitudes, however, changed markedly during the 1960s when parents were bombarded with professional and semiprofessional dicta on the importance of learning in the early years. If you did not start teaching children when they were young, parents were told, a golden opportunity for learning would be lost. Today, tax-supported kindergartens are operating in almost every state, and children are admitted at increasingly earlier ages. (In many cities a child born before January 1 can enter kindergarten the preceding September, making his or her effective entrance age four.) Once enrolled in kindergarten, children are now often presented with formal instruction in reading and math once reserved for the later grades.

How did this radical turnabout in attitudes happen? There are probably many reasons, but a major one was the attack on "progressive" education that occurred in the fifties and that found much education material dated. The Russian launching of the Sputnik in 1957 drove Americans into a frenzy of self-criticism about education and promoted the massive curriculum movement of the 1960s that brought academics from major universities into curriculum writing. Unfortunately, many academics knew their discipline but didn't know children and were unduly optimistic about how fast and how much children could learn. This optimism was epitomized in Jerome Bruner's famous phrase, "That any subject can be taught effectively in some intellectually honest form to any child at any stage of development."[9] What a shift from "early ripe, early rot"!

The trend toward early academic pressure was further supported by the civil rights movement, which highlighted the poor performance of disadvantaged children in our schools. Teachers were under attack by avant-garde educators such as John Holt[10], Jonathan Kozol[11], and Herbert Kohl[12], and they were forced to defend their lack of success by shifting the blame. Their children did not do well because they came inadequately prepared. It was not what was going on in the classroom but what had not gone on at home that was the root of academic failure among the disadvantaged; hence Headstart, hence busing, which by integrating students would equalize background differences.

One consequence of all this concern for the early years was the demise of the "readiness" concept. The concept of readiness had been extolled by developmental psychologists such as Arnold Gesell who argued for the biological limitations on learning.[13] Gesell believed that children were not biologically ready for learning to read until they had attained a Mental Age (a test score in which children are credited with a certain number of months for each correct answer) of six and one-half years. But the emphasis on early intervention and early intellectual stimulation (even of infants) made the

7

concept of readiness appear dated and old-fashioned. In professional educational circles readiness, once an honored educational concept, is now in disrepute.

The pressure for early academic achievement is but one of many contemporary pressures on children to grow up fast. Children's dress is another. Three or four decades ago, prepubescent boys wore short pants and knickers until they began to shave; getting a pair of long pants was a true rite of passage. Girls were not permitted to wear makeup or sheer stockings until they were in their teens. For both sexes, clothing set children apart. It signaled adults that these people were to be treated differently, perhaps indulgently; it made it easier for children to act as children. Today even preschool children wear miniature versions of adult clothing. From overalls to LaCoste shirts to scaled-down designer fashions, a whole range of adult costumes is available to children. (Along with them is a wide choice of corresponding postures such as those of young teenagers modeling designer jeans.) Below is an illustration from a recent article by Susan Ferraro entitled "Hotsy Totsy."

> *It was a party like any other: ice cream and cake, a donkey poster and twelve haphazard tails, and a door prize for everyone including Toby, the birthday girl's little brother who couldn't do anything but smear icing.*

> *"Ooh," sighed seven-year-old Melissa as she opened her first present. It was Calvin Klein jeans. "Aah," she gasped as the second box revealed a bright new top from Gloria Vanderbilt. There were Christian Dior undies from grandma—a satiny little chemise and matching bloomer bottoms—and mother herself had fallen for a marvelous party outfit from Yves St. Laurent. Melissa's best friend gave her an Izod sports shirt, complete with alligator emblem. Added to that a couple of books were, indeed, very nice and predictable—except for the fancy doll one guest's eccentric mother insisted on bringing.[14]*

When children dress like adults they are more likely to behave as adults do, to imitate adult actions. It is hard to walk like an adult male wearing corduroy knickers that make an awful noise. But boys in long pants can walk like men, and little girls in tight jeans can walk like women. It is more difficult today to recognize that children are children and not miniature adults, because children dress and move like adults.

Another evidence of the pressure to grow up fast is the change in the programs of summer camps for children. Although there are still many summer camps that offer swimming, sailing, horseback riding, archery, and camp fires—activities we remember from our own childhood—an increasing number of summer camps offer specialized training in many different areas, including foreign languages, tennis, baseball, dance, music, and even computers.

Among such camps the most popular seem to be those that specialize in competitive sports: softball, weight training, tennis, golf, football, basketball, hockey, soccer, lacrosse, gymnastics, wrestling, judo, figure skating, surfing. "Whatever the sport there's a camp (or ten or a hundred of them) dedicated to teaching the finer points. Often these camps are under the direction, actual or nominal, of a big name in a particular sport, and many have professional athletes on their staffs. The daily routine is rigorous, with individual and/or group lessons, practice sessions and tournaments, complete with trophies. And, to cheer the athletes on with more pep and polish, cheerleaders and song girls can also attend."[15]

The change in the programs of summer camps reflects the new attitude that the years of childhood are not to be frittered away by engaging in activities merely for fun. Rather, the years are to be used to perfect skills and abilities that are the same as those of adults. Children are early initiated into the rigors of adult competition. Competitive sports for children are becoming ever more widespread and include everything from Little League to Pee Wee hockey. The pressure to engage in organized, competitive sports at camp and at home is one of the most obvious pressures on contemporary children to grow up fast.

There are many other pressures as well. Many children today travel across the country, and indeed across the world, alone. The so-called unaccompanied minor has become so commonplace that airlines have instituted special rules and regulations for them. The phenomenon is a direct result of the increase in middle-class divorces and the fact that one or the other parent moves to another part of the country or world. Consequently, the child travels to visit one parent or the other. Children also fly alone to see grandparents or to go to special camps or training facilities.

9

While some children really do not like to travel alone, others enjoy it. This young man's story is illustrative:

> *Louic Villeneuve, nine, who lives in Cambridge, flies to Montreal alone each summer to visit his mother and to stay in the city where he spent the first five years of his life. "He loves it," said his father. "Once there weren't enough seats in the back of the plane so I had to go first class," Louic said, "there was so much food." The only problem Louic finds is adults who ask him which he likes better, Montreal or Boston. No matter which he answers, Louic has found, someone is unhappy. When his father flew with him recently, Louic commented, "I wish you weren't with me." A child alone, he seems to have discovered, gets more attention, more crayons, and more food than one travelling with a parent.*[16]

Although airline personnel take good care of unaccompanied children and some children like Louic enjoy traveling alone, it is very stressful for other children. Young children in particular may feel that they are abandoning their parent, or are being abandoned, or both. Being in an airplane with strange people and going to a different living arrangement, children are required to make adaptations that are more appropriate to older children and adults.

Other facets of society also press children to grow up fast. Lawyers, for example, are encouraging children to sue their parents for a variety of grievances. In California, four-and-one-half-year-old Kimberely Ann Alpin, who was born out of wedlock, is suing her father for the right to visit with him. The father, who provides support payments, does not want to see Kimberely. Whatever the decision, or the merits of the case, it illustrates the tendency of child-advocates to accord adult legal rights to children. In West Hartford, Connecticut, David Burn, age 16, legally "divorced" his parents under a new state law in 1980. While such rights may have some benefits, they also put children in a difficult and often stressful position vis-à-vis their parents.

The media too, including music, books, films, and television, increasingly portray young people as precocious and present them in more or less explicit sexual or manipulative situations. Such portrayals force children to think they should act grown up before they are ready. In the movie *Little Darlings* the two principals—teenage girls—are in competition as to who will lose her virginity first. Similarly, teen music extols songs such as "Take Your Time (Do It Right)" and "Do That to Me One More Time," which are high on the charts of teen favorites. Television also promotes teenage erotica with features detailing such themes as teenage prostitution. According to some teenagers, the only show on television where playing hard to get is not regarded as stupid is "Laverne and Shirley."

The media promote not only teenage sexuality but also the wearing of adult clothes and the use of adult behaviors, language, and interpersonal strategies. Sexual promotion occurs in the context of other suggestions and models for growing up fast. A Jordache jean commercial, which depicts a young girl piggyback on a young boy, highlights clothing and implicit sexuality as well as adult expressions, hairstyles, and so on. Likewise, in the film *Foxes*, four teenage girls not only blunder into sexual entanglements but also model provocative adult clothing, makeup, language, and postures. Thus the media reinforce the pressure on children to grow up fast in their language, thinking, and behavior.

But can young people be hurried into growing up fast emotionally as well? Psychologists and psychiatrists recognize that emotions and feelings are the most complex and intricate part of development. Feelings and emotions have their own timing and rhythm and cannot be hurried. Young teenagers may look and behave like adults but they usually don't feel like adults. (Watch a group of teenagers in a children's playground as they swing on the swings and teeter on the teeter-totters). Children can grow up fast in some ways but not in others. Growing up emotionally is complicated and difficult under any circumstances but may be especially so when children's behavior and appearance speak "adult" while their feelings cry "child."

THE CHILD INSIDE

Some of the more negative consequences of hurrying usually become evident in adolescence, when the pressures to grow up fast collide with institutional prohibitions. Children pushed to grow up fast suddenly find that many adult prerogatives—which they assumed would be their prerogative—such as smoking, drinking, driving, and so on, are denied them until they reach a certain age.

Many adolescents feel betrayed by a society that tells them to grow up fast but also to remain a child. Not surprisingly, the stresses of growing up fast often result in troubled and troublesome behavior during adolescence.

In a recent article, Patricia O'Brien gave some examples of what she called "the shrinking of childhood." Her examples reflect a rush to experiment that is certainly one consequence of growing up fast:

> *Martin L (not his real name) confronted his teenager who had stayed out very late the night before. The son replied, "Look, Dad, I've done it all—drugs, sex, and booze, there is nothing left I don't know about." This young man is twelve years old!*

> *In Washington, D.C. area schools administrators estimate that many thousands of teenagers are alcoholics, with an estimated 30,000 such young people in Northern Virginia alone.*[17]

The rush to experiment is perhaps most noticeable in teenage sexual behavior. Although survey data are not always as reliable as one might wish, the available information suggests that there has been a dramatic increase in the number of sexually active teenage girls in the last decade. Melvin Zelnick and John F. Kanther, professors of public health at Johns Hopkins University in Baltimore, conclude that nearly 50 percent of the total population of teenage girls between the ages of fifteen and nineteen (about 10.3 million females) have had premarital sex. The percentage has nearly doubled since the investigators first undertook their study in 1971. "Things that supported remaining a virgin in the past—the fear of getting pregnant, being labelled the 'town pump,' or whatever have disappeared," observes Zelnick.[18]

Young people themselves are very much aware of this trend. "I'd say half the girls in my graduating class are virgins," says an eighteen-year-old high school senior from New Iberia, Louisiana. "But you wouldn't believe those freshmen and sophomores. By the time they graduate there aren't going to be any virgins left."[19]

There are a number of disturbing consequences of this sexual liberation. The number of teenage pregnancies is growing at a startling rate. About 10 percent of all teenage girls, one million in all, get pregnant each year and the number keeps increasing. About 600,000 teenagers give birth each year, and the sharpest increase in such births is for girls under fourteen! In addition, venereal disease is a growing problem among teenagers, who account for 25 percent of the one million or so cases of gonorrhea each year.

The causes of this enhanced sexual activity among young people today are many and varied. The age of first menstruation, for example, has dropped from age seventeen about a century ago to age twelve and a half today. Fortunately this seems to be the lower limit made possible by good health care and nutrition. However, this age of first menstruation has remained stable over the past decade, so it cannot account for the increased sexual activity of young women during this period. Other contributing factors include rapid changes in social values, women's liberation, the exploding divorce rate, the decline of parental and institutional authority, and the fatalistic sense, not often verbalized, that we are all going to die in a nuclear holocaust anyway, so "what the hell, have a good time."

Although the media are quick to pick up these sexual trends and exploit them for commercial purposes (for example, the cosmetics for girls four to nine years old currently being marketed by toy manufacturers), the immediate adult model is perhaps the most powerful and the most pervasive. Married couples are generally discreet about their sexuality in front of their offspring—in part because of a natural tendency to avoid exposing children to what they might not understand, but also because by the time the children are born, much of the romantic phase of the relationship for many couples is in the past.

But single parents who are dating provide a very different model for children. Quite aside from confrontations such as that in *Kramer vs. Kramer* wherein the son encounters the father's naked girlfriend, single parents are likely to be much more overtly sexual than married couples. With single parents, children may witness the romantic phase of courtship—the hand-holding, the eye-gazing, the constant touching and fondling. This overt sexuality, with all the positive affection it demonstrates, may encourage young people to look for something similar.

It is also true, as Professor Mavis Hetherington of the University of Virginia has found in her research, that daughters of divorced women tend to be more sexually oriented, more flirtatious with men than daughters of widowed mothers or daughters from two-parent homes.[20] Because there are more teenage daughters from single-parent homes today than ever before, this too could contribute to enhanced sexual activity of contemporary teenage girls.

While it is true that some young people in every past generation have engaged in sex at an early age, have become pregnant, contracted venereal disease, and so on, they were always a small proportion of the population. What is new today are the numbers, which indicate that pressures to grow up fast are social and general rather than familial and specific (reflecting parental biases and needs). The proportion of young people who are abusing drugs, are sexually active, and are becoming pregnant is so great that we must look to the society as a whole for a full explanation, not to just the parents who mirror it.

Parallelling the increased sexuality of young people is an increase in children of what in adults are known as stress diseases. Pediatricians report a greater incidence of such ailments as headaches, stomachaches, allergic reactions, and so on in today's youngsters than in previous generations. Type A behavior (high-strung, competitive, demanding) has been identified in children and associated with heightened cholesterol levels. It has also been associated with parental pressure for achievement.

Another negative reflection of the pressure to grow up fast is teenage (and younger) crime. During 1980, for example, New York police arrested 12,762 children aged sixteen and under on felony charges. In Chicago the figure for the same period was 18,754 charges. Having worked for juvenile courts, I am sure that these figures are underestimated. Many children who have committed felonies are released without a formal complaint so that they will not have a police record. The children who are "booked" have usually had several previous encounters with the law.

The following examples, recent cases from the New York Police Department, illustrate the sort of activities for which children get arrested:

- On 27 February 1981, a boy who had to stand on tiptoes to speak to the bank teller made off with $118 that he had secured at gunpoint. He was nine years old, the youngest felon ever sought by the F.B.I.

14

- A ten-year-old Brooklyn girl was apprehended in December after she snatched a wallet from a woman's purse. Police said it was the girl's nineteenth arrest.
- One of four suspects captured in the murder of a policeman in Queens on 12 January 1981 was a fifteen-year-old youth.
- A thirteen-year-old Bronx boy was arrested in March 1981 on charges that he killed two elderly women during attempted purse snatchings.
- Another thirteen-year-old boy had a record of thirty-two arrests when seized last year on a charge of attempted murder. He later confessed to an incredible 200 plus felonies.[21]

Such crimes are not being committed just by poor disadvantaged youth who are acting out against a society prejudiced against them. Much teenage crime is committed by middle-class youngsters. However, it tends to be concealed because police and parents try to protect the children; but sometimes this is not possible. One case involved a thirteen-year-old Long Island boy who was killed by three teenagers who stomped on him and strangled him by stuffing stones down his throat. He was attacked because he accidentally discovered that the other boys had stolen an old dirt bike worth only a couple of dollars. It was one of the most brutal and gruesome murders to be committed on Long Island.

How can pressure to grow up fast contribute to crime among teenagers from affluent backgrounds? Consider the case of John Warnock Hinckley, Jr., the young man who shot President Reagan and others on March 31, 1981. Unlike other assassins such as Lee Harvey Oswald who shot President Kennedy, John Hinckley came from a respected upper-class family. Young Hinckley's father had built a prosperous business, and he and his wife had brought up three bright children. The family was religious, law-abiding, and socially conscious. Before and after the family moved from Dallas to Denver, Mrs. Hinckley made it a point to stay home to raise the children. Mr. Hinckley, though busy with his business, always made it a point to take his children camping, on family outings, and the like.

> *In line with this model upbringing, the three children—especially Scott, the eldest, now 32—and Diane, now 29—were viewed as popular, intelligent and good looking. Scott, for example, was a scholarly athlete at Highland Park High*

15

*School, the most prestigious public high school in the
Dallas area. He was a member of an academic honorary
group, the student council and the chess club and he was a
varsity tennis player. At Vanderbilt University in Nashville,
Tenn., Scott the fraternity man earned academic honors in
mechanical engineering and went on to become the Singa-
pore branch manager of Reading & Bates Inc. a Tulsa
based oil company.*

*Diane is just as memorable. The blond beauty was the head
cheerleader, a home-coming princess, an honor student,
and a member of the choir and of the student council
during her years at Highland Park High. At well-heeled
Southern Methodist University in Dallas, she joined a
sorority, majored in education, and met her future husband, Stephen Sims, who now is a Dallas insurance execu-
tive. Friends describe her today as a "model housewife"
with two small children, a red brick house, and a two-car
garage.*[22]

John Hinckley also did well in his early school career. He was
active in sports and in the Cub Scouts. In the eighth grade, he was
too small to make the basketball team but he handed out towels and
led cheers from the bench. In the seventh and ninth grades he was
elected president of his homeroom. But the pressure of Highland
Park High School was apparently too much for John. From an outgoing cheerful boy, he became progressively more quiet and withdrawn, eventually preferring to practice his guitar alone at home
than to be out with his friends.

Unlike his brother and sister, who went to expensive private
schools, John elected to go to Texas Tech, a public institution. But
he did not fraternize and often enrolled in courses that he never
attended. Tendencies toward political extremism began to emerge.
John joined and was eventually expelled from the Naturalist
Socialist Party of America (a neo-Nazi party). He was expelled from
the group because, according to another member, "We thought he
was either deranged or could become an agent provocateur of violence."

John left college, was out of touch with his parents, and began
the aimless drifting that was suddenly given direction and motiva-

tion by the desire to shoot the President. That this act was to gain the attention of a movie actress may be true in part, but the actress also had the same first name as his mother—Jodi.

John Hinckley's case shows how the pressure to achieve and to achieve early can bring about personality disorder and emotional disturbance. Had John been born into a different family, had his brother and sister not been so successful, he might have found himself. But, in Erik Erikson's terms, John's older brother—by being at the same time athlete, scholar, and social leader—preempted all of the personal identities held out as valuable by his parents. Consequently, John adopted a negative identity—one of extremism, aloneness, social disruption—the negative of what his parents valued.[23]

The pressure to grow up fast, to achieve early in the area of sports, academics, and social interaction, is very great in middle-class America. There is no room today for the "late bloomers," the children who come into their own later in life rather than earlier (John might have been one of these). Children have to achieve success early or they are regarded as losers. It has gone so far that many parents refuse to have their children repeat or be retained in kindergarten—despite all the evidence that this is the best possible time to retain a child. "But," the parents say, "how can we tell our friends that our son failed kindergarten?"

John Hinckley's solution to the problem of early achievement and success was attaining notoriety, catching people's attention with negative rather than positive accomplishments. But there are many other solutions to this pressure to achieve early. One such solution is to join a cult, such as the "Moonies." What characterizes such cults is that they accept young people unconditionally, regardless of academic success or failure. The cults, in effect, provide an accepting family that does not demand achievement in return for love, although cults do demand obedience and adherence to a certain moral ethic. Even rebellious young people find it easy to adhere to these rules in the atmosphere of acceptance and lack of pressure and competition offered by the cult group. Cult membership is another form of negative identity in which young people adopt a group identity rather than an individual one.

A case in point is the Christ Commune (a pseudonym), a branch of the best-organized and most rapidly growing sect of what has been called the Jesus movement. The Commune is a summer camp where members come from their homes for a few months each year.

The population (about one hundred) consists of young adults between the ages of fifteen and thirty (average age twenty-one) who are white and come from large (four to eight children), middle-class families. Most have completed high school and some have done college work. One gets the impression they are young people who have not distinguished themselves socially, academically, or athletically and who have held boring, low-paying jobs.

The group offers a strict moral code, a rigid behavioral program, and a sense of mission, of being chosen by and working for God through the mediation of Christ. The members work hard—they get up at 4:30 A.M. and go to sleep at 11:00 P.M. They seem happy with simple food (little meat, water to drink, peanut butter sandwiches for lunch) and strenuous work six days a week. Entertainment and recreation are limited to sitting in a common room, talking, singing spirituals, and engaging in spontaneous prayer.

Such communes, the Jesus movement, and other religious groups are attractive to young people whose personal styles are at variance with those of the larger society. Such groups offer recognition and status to young people who tend to be noncompetitive, anti-intellectual, and spiritual in orientation. Thus the groups provide a needed haven from the pressure to grow up fast, to achieve early, and to make a distinctive mark in life.

The last phenomenon in relation to hurrying to be discussed here is teenage suicide. Currently, suicide is the third leading cause of death during the teen years—preceded only by death via accidents and homicide. An American Academy of Pediatrics report on teenage suicide indicates a large increase in the number of suicides by adolescents in the last decade—the number is now about 5000 per year. For young people between the ages of fifteen to nineteen, the number of suicides per year doubled during the period from 1968 to 1976. The data for young adolescents of ages ten to fourteen are even more distressing: the number of suicides was 116 in 1968 and rose to 158 by 1976.

For every suicide completed, some 50 to 200 are attempted but not successful. Adolescents from all walks of life, all races, religions, and ethnic groups commit or attempt to commit suicide. Boys are generally more successful than girls because they use more lethal methods—boys tend to shoot or hang themselves whereas girls are more likely to overdose on pills or to cut their wrists. "For most adolescents," the pediatric report concludes, "suicide represents an attempt to resolve a difficult conflict, escape an intolerable living arrangement or punish important individuals in their lives."

To illustrate how hurrying can contribute to teenage suicide, consider the data from the most affluent suburbs of Chicago, a ten-mile stretch of communities along Chicago's northside lakefront that is one of the richest areas in the country. It is the locale chosen by director Robert Redford for the movie *Ordinary People*. The median income per family is about $60,000. Children in these areas attend excellent schools, travel about the world on vacations, are admitted to the best and most prestigious private colleges, and often drive their own cars (which can sometimes be a Mercedes). These are children of affluence who would seem to have it made.

And yet, this cluster of suburbs has the highest number of teenage suicides per year in the state, and almost in the nation. There has been a 250 percent increase in suicides per year over the past decade. These figures are dismaying not only in and of themselves but because the community has made serious efforts at suicide prevention, including the training of teachers in suicide detection and the provision of a twenty-four-hour hot line. One hot line, provided by Chicago psychoanalyst Joseph Pribyl, receives some 150 calls per month. But the suicides continue.

A nineteen-year-old from Glencoe, Illinois, says, "We have an outrageous number of suicides for a community our size." One of this teenager's friends cut her wrist and two others drove their cars into trees. "Growing up here you are handed everything on a platter, but something else is missing. The one thing parents don't give is love, understanding, and acceptance of you as a person." And Isadora Sherman, of Highland Park's Jewish Family and Community Service says, "People give their kids a lot materially, but expect a lot in return. No one sees his kids as average, and those who don't perform are made to feel like failures."[24]

Chicago psychiatrist Harold Visotsky succinctly states how pressure to achieve at an early age, to grow up and be successful fast can contribute to teenage suicide: "People on the lower end of the social scale expect less than these people. Whatever anger the poor experience is acted out in antisocial ways—vandalism, homicide, riots—and the sense of shared misery in the lower income groups prevents people from feeling so isolated. With well-to-do kids, *the rattle goes in the mouth and the foot goes on the social ladder.* The competition ethic takes over, making a child feel even more alone. He's more likely to take it out on himself than society."[25]

Adolescents are very audience conscious. Failure is a public event, and the adolescent senses the audience's disapproval. It is the sense that "everyone knows" that is so painful and that can lead to attempted and successful suicides in adolescents who are otherwise so disposed. Hurrying our children has, I believe, contributed to the extraordinary rise in suicide rates among young people over the past decade.

ALL GROWN UP AND NO PLACE TO GO

Sigmund Freud was once asked to describe the characteristics of maturity, and he replied: *lieben und arbeiten* ("loving and working"). The mature adult is one who can love and allow himself or herself to be loved and who can work productively, meaningfully, and with satisfaction. Yet most adolescents, and certainly all children, are really not able to work or to love in the mature way that Freud had in mind. Children love their parents in a far different way from how they will love a real or potential mate. And many, probably most, young people will not find their life work until they are well into young adulthood.

When children are expected to dress, act, and think as adults, they are really being asked to playact, because all of the trappings of adulthood do not in any way make them adults in the true sense of *lieben und arbeiten.* It is ironic that the very parents who won't allow their children to believe in Santa Claus or the Easter Bunny (because they are fantasy and therefore dishonest) allow their children to dress and behave as adults without any sense of the tremendous dishonesty involved in allowing children to present themselves in this grown-up way.

It is even more ironic that practices once considered the province of lower-class citizens now have the allure of middle-class chic. Divorce, single parenting, dual-career couples, and unmarried couples living together were common among the lower class decades ago. Such arrangements were prompted more often than not by economic need, and the children of low-income families were thus pressured to grow up fast out of necessity. They were pitied and looked down upon by upper- and middle-class parents, who helped provide shelters like the Home for Little Wanderers in Boston.

Today the middle class has made divorce its status symbol. And single parenting and living together without being married are increasingly commonplace. Yet middle-class children have not kept pace with the adjustments these adult changes require. In years past a child in a low-income family could appreciate the need to take on adult responsibilities early; families needed the income a child's farm or factory labor would bring, and chores and child-rearing tasks had to be allocated to even younger members of the family. But for the middle-income child today, it is hard to see the necessity of being relegated to a baby sitter or sent to a nursery school or a day care center when he or she has a perfectly nice playroom and yard at home. It isn't the fact of parents' being divorced that is so distressing to middle-class children, but rather that often it seems so unnecessary, so clearly a reflection of parent and not child need. As we shall see, it is the feeling of being used, of being exploited by parents, of losing the identity and uniqueness of childhood without just cause that constitute the major stress of hurrying and account for so much unhappiness among affluent young people today.

It is certainly true that the trend toward obscuring the divisions between children and adults is part of a broad egalitarian movement in this country that seeks to overcome the barriers separating the sexes, ethnic and racial groups, and the handicapped. We see these trends in unisex clothing and hairstyles, in the call for equal pay for equal work, in the demands for affirmative action, and in the appeals and legislation that provide the handicapped with equal opportunities for education and meaningful jobs.

From this perspective, the contemporary pressure for children to grow up fast is only one symptom of a much larger social phenomenon in this country—a movement toward true equality, toward the ideal expressed in our Declaration of Independence. While one can only applaud this movement with respect to the sexes, ethnic and racial groups, and the handicapped, its unthinking extension to children is unfortunate.

Children need time to grow, to learn, and to develop. To treat them differently from adults is not to discriminate against them but rather to recognize their special estate. Similarly, when we provide bilingual programs for Hispanic children, we are not discriminating against them but are responding to the special needs they have, which, if not attended to, would prevent them from attaining a successful education and true equality. In the same way, building ramps for handicapped students is a means to their attaining equal opportunity. Recognizing special needs is not discriminatory; on the contrary, it is the only way that true equality can be attained.

All children have, vis-à-vis adults, special needs—intellectual, social, and emotional. Children do not learn, think, or feel in the same way as adults. To ignore these differences, to treat children as adults, is really not democratic or egalitarian. If we ignore the special needs of children, we are behaving just as if we denied Hispanic or Indian children bilingual programs, or denied the handicapped their ramps and guideposts. In truth, the recognition of a group's special needs and accommodation to those needs are the only true ways to insure equality and true equal opportunity.

Chapter 2

The Dynamics of Hurrying: Parents

Americans have traditionally employed two contrasting metaphors for childhood. The first of these, perhaps originating in our nation's agricultural-rural past, describes the child as a growing plant that needs to be nourished and looked after but that nevertheless may be trusted to unfold according to its own inner dynamic of growth. In this metaphor the child absorbs the surrounding world and takes it into himself or herself. Walt Whitman captures this "imbibing" process consummately in *Leaves of Grass:*

> *The schooners, the waves, the clouds,*
> *the flying sea crow, the fragrance*
> *of saltmarsh and mud, the horizon's edge.*
> *These became part of that child who went forth everyday*
> *And who now goes and will always go forth everyday.*[1]

The best formulated scientific version of the plant metaphor is that offered by the late Jean Piaget, who saw the child's intellectual development as part of the ongoing larger process of biological adaptation. For Piaget, human intelligence is thus best understood as an extension of this adaptation. Thinking, like digestion, transforms incoming information in a way that is useful to the individual. But thinking, like vision, also adapts to the constraints of the surrounding world. Like a plant or an organism, thinking both changes and is changed by the environment.[2]

Another metaphor—equally old and intellectually honorable—construes the child in physicalist rather than biological terms. The sixteenth-century English philosopher John Locke gave this view its classic formulation when he spoke of the child as a *tabula rasa*, or blank slate (tablet), upon which life experience is written.[3] Our modern industrial age has given a slightly different twist to the Lockean formulation; we see the child as a kind of "raw material" to be molded and shaped by parents, education, and social institutions. John Watson, the psychologist credited with founding the school of behaviorism, epitomized this approach in his boast, "Give me a dozen healthy infants and I'll guarantee to take any one at random and train him to become a doctor, a lawyer, artist, merchant, beggarman, thief."[4] A similar boast echoes through the pages of B. F. Skinner's bestseller of the fifties, *Walden Two*, a book that introduced the concept of "engineering" the behavior of children (and indeed of all human beings in a society) along "adaptive" and "healthy" lines.[5]

The two metaphors, then—the child as growing organism with its own emergent identity and the child as malleable material awaiting society's imprinting—abide with us, representative perhaps of the two discrete social economies, agricultural and industrial, of our past and present. In contemporary America, those who work regularly with children—teachers, counselors, caretakers—tend to adopt the metaphor of the growing organism. They envision the school, thus, as a farm where living things grow freely, each according to his or her own rhythm and season. On the other hand, it is not surprising that the denizens of government (administrators, law-enforcement officials, juvenile authorities, and so forth) prefer the view of children as malleable entities awaiting the imposition of form from without. From their perspective, schools are less farms than factories, and the child in question is less a tree than an assembly-line product, predictably fashioned and quantitatively measured.

And yet perhaps both metaphors are already dated, for even as we pause to observe and describe our society, it is changing around us. We have, for example, already developed an economy where both farm and factory employ a far smaller percentage of the work force than formerly. The number of people employed in the vast service sector of our economy now exceeds in size the old industrial proletariat of the early twentieth century. Robots, automatization, and miniaturization render the traditional labor-intensive factory (and factory worker) obsolete, much as enormous tractors, combines, sprayers, and reapers have radically and permanently altered the agricultural landscape. High technology, genetic engineering, and information processing utilize different talents, strategies, and facilities than does the traditional factory or farm.

Such developments cannot fail to affect our views of self and family. As we move into the postindustrial era, we will certainly fashion appropriate metaphors to conceive childhood. And it is very much within this context of a changing society, economy, and family and value structure that we must view our new-found propensity for hurrying children to grow up fast. As yet we lack a metaphor to describe this hurried view of child-rearing, but unfortunately we have the thing itself. One possibility, of course, is that in a time of straightened economic circumstances, we are reappropriating the medieval view of seeing children only as miniature adults ready to enter the work force. The increase in child abuse and exploitation today (also characteristic of the middle ages) would tend to support this hypothesis, as would the increase of adult crimes (theft, robbery, murder) committed by children. On the other hand, despite its apparent relevancy, such a view neglects the profound truth that we are not innocent about children—as our medieval forebears perhaps were—nor are our economy and society primitive. Disingenuous in some degree, we are not innocent. To be sure, we harass our children with some of the emotional-intellectual-social demands of adulthood yet at the same time we treat them—often ostentatiously—as mere children. Sometimes we go so far as to infantilize them (even adolescents) by permitting them to have messy rooms, to leave things lying about, to get up at odd hours, and to eat junk food. We thus recognize children's special estate at the very same time that we hurry them to grow up fast.

What are the ways parents hurry children? And what powerful motivations and distractions cause us to disregard the mountain of knowledge we have about childhood and child development, about the special needs and identity of young people?

The beginning of an answer lies in the theme that was touched upon earlier: rapid change. The bewildering rapidity and profound extent of ongoing social change are the unique hallmarks of our era, setting us apart from every previous society. For us, in the foreseeable future, nothing is permanent. Stress is an organism's reaction to this change, this impermanence. We live, therefore, in a time of widespread, deep-seated stress; it is a companion that is so constant we may easily forget how completely stress pervades our lives.

While we shall later examine the concept of stress in greater detail, I will here point to three particular sources of stress for parents as adults that have flourished dramatically in recent years. First, we are more afraid: the threat of violence, theft, and intimidation is now a permanent possibility in life in urban America. Every inhabitant of a major city (and many suburban and exurbanites as well) knows someone who has experienced, or has personally experienced, physical attack in some form.

We are more alone: separation and divorce statistics have reached new highs; and while some people choose to live alone and feel most comfortable in solitude, there are more people today who live alone because they are unable to find a suitable partner.

We are more professionally insecure: the threats of technological unemployment, inflation, recession, rising prices, and so on are also prevalent.

People in stress, like those in ill health, are absorbed with themselves—the demands on them, their reactions and feelings, their hydra-headed anxieties. They are, in a word, egocentric, though not necessarily conceited or prideful. They have little opportunity to consider the needs and interests of others. This state of affairs has not gone unnoticed—far from it. Social critic Tom Wolfe minted the apt phrase "me decade" to describe the absorption with "personal potential" that characterized the sixties and early seventies.[6] Historian Christopher Lasch has labelled our society "the culture of narcissism"—narcissism, in psychoanalytic theory, is the attachment of the self to the self as to a primary love object.[7] It is likely that today's much-noted self-centeredness is, in large part, a response to the stress of living in a society where inconstancy is the only constant and where the needed roots and abiding familiarities of life—private and public—are easily eradicated or never develop in the first place.

The prevalence of self-centeredness puts us squarely in a dilemma in regard to raising children. If it is to be done well, child-rearing requires, more than most activities of life, a good deal of decentering from one's own needs and perspectives. Such decentering is relatively easy when a society is stable and when there is an extended, supportive structure that the parent can depend upon. The traditional cultures of Japan and China offer fine examples: a well-defined, stable social structure freed parents from the stress of adapting to constant social change and instead permitted them to focus their adaptive powers on the growing and changing children in their midst.

But consider the male adult in contemporary America. In an economy distorted by inflation, infiltrated by computerization, miniaturization, and automation, pressed grimly by foreign imports, he may well fear for his job. If he is employed in a metropolis of the old, industrial Northeast, he now wonders whether he will have to learn a new occupation or skill and relocate to a new city or state, leaving behind the security and network of friends and family. Many of his friends are divorced, separated, or having affairs, and he wonders whether his life won't follow in suit. His church may be giving him conflicting messages—if he is Catholic, for example, his local priest may be saying one thing about birth control and sex, and the Vatican may be saying another. Whom to believe? What to cleave to? He never stops hearing about crime and inflation statistics, or the growing danger of nuclear proliferation and the possibility of world war or environmental disaster. He worries about the negative health effects of food additives, coffee, saccharine, cholesterol, red meat, and any one of a hundred common consumer items.

Or consider the single mother who is trying to raise three children with little or no financial support from a former husband. (Half of the children in the current generation are likely to live in households headed by single parents.) Such women are concerned not only about finances and the welfare of their children but also about being alone when the children are grown. Add to this the fact that working women are still paid less than men, are too often harassed sexually on the job, and have trouble getting financial credit on their own.

Such a man, such a woman—their numbers are increasing in our society—may expend so much effort coping with the daily stress of living that there is little strength or enthusiasm left over for parenting. They—we—are unable to put our knowledge about children into practice. We hurry children because stress induces us to put our own needs ahead of their needs.

Parents may justify their actions by reverting to the metaphor of the "infinitely malleable" child. Caught up in our own coping struggle, inundated with the multifarious demands of life, we prefer to think of our children as endlessly flexible and resilient materials. As such, they may therefore be expected to adapt easily to our (adult) needs, schedules, interests, perspectives. We expect them to adapt more to adult life programs than we adapt to their child life programs. Yet the opposed metaphor of the child as growing plant also has dangers. It may lead to a romantic conception of childhood as a time free of conflict, fear, struggle, or demand. This, in its own way, is just as dangerous a notion as the contrasting one of infinite malleability, and it has led to the overpermissiveness that is nearly as much the hallmark of our era as hurrying.

Specifically, then, how do parental stress and the metaphor of child as raw material become transmuted into hurrying? We have seen how adults under stress become self-centered and therefore have considerably more trouble in seeing other people in all the complexity of their individual personalities. People under stress tend to see other people in the shorthand of symbols, not the often hard-to-decipher longhand of personhood. Under stress, we see others as certain obvious, easily grasped stereotypes and abstractions. When we are ill, other people often symbolize health; when we are fearful, others appear intrepid and courageous; when we are depressed, life seems to present us with nothing but the happy-go-lucky. While we (or they) may imagine that we react to them as John, Mary, and Fred, we are in fact treating them as simplistic stereotypes, and this is because we are too wrapped up in our own illness, fear, or depression. Thus with our children; it is as objects or symbols—not as full subjects—that we hurry them.

Why do people under stress have recourse to symbols? To what end do they use them? Basically, people under stress are not only self-centered, they also lack energy for dealing with issues apart from themselves. Symbols, oversimplifications really, are energy-conserving. Parents under stress see their children as symbols because it is the least demanding way to deal with them. A student, a skater, a tennis player, a confidant are clear-cut symbols, easy guides for what to think, to see, and how to behave. Symbols thus free the parent from the energy consuming task of knowing the child as a totality, a whole person. Symbols also conserve energy in another way. They are ready-at-hand targets for projecting unfulfilled needs, feelings, and emotions. Thus, by treating children as symbols, parents conserve the energy needed for coping with stress and have ready-made screens for projecting some of the consequences of stress, fear, anxiety, and frustration. Such energy conservation, however, is really not "cost-beneficial," for in treating our children as symbols—in hurrying them—we harm them and, ultimately, ourselves.

THE CHILD AS SURROGATE SELF

Parents who go to work—which is to say, almost all fathers and many mothers—are under more stress today than at any time since the Great Depression. In many businesses, human beings are being displaced by machines (for example, in computer printing, the honorable profession of linotype operator has been all but eliminated.) Many blue-collar workers must confront the reality that they will have to learn a new trade. Their counterparts in the white-collar professions encounter harrowing job insecurity as companies' fortunes rise and fall with inflation, lowered productivity, undependable government contracts, and so on. The anxiety created by such circumstances is an obvious form of stress.

Moreover, the joy and team spirit of work relations in many industries have disappeared. Professor Lester Thurow of the Massachusetts Institute of Technology credits the competitive edge that Japan and Germany have over the United States for the flourishing of cooperation and *esprit de corps* in these countries. He points out that "many workers in Japan receive a third income from bonuses based on company profits, a form of compensation U.S. labor has been loath to accept."[8] And Akio Morita, chairman and co-founder of Sony, says, "Teamwork historically is, I think, the American way. But your managers soon forgot that. They got greedy; they viewed the worker as a tool. That has not been good for the American products or American companies, and it has hurt your competitive stature in the world."[9] It is also not good for worker satisfaction. The dog-eat-dog atmosphere in the U.S. work place is oppressive and conducive of general dissatisfaction among employees.

Similar problems occur among white collar workers. I recently met with a number of school administrators from an affluent Northeastern suburb. Their story echoed that of others I had heard from such groups across the United States and Canada. These men and women were in their thirties and early forties and were good at what they did, but they saw little chance for advancement and, in any case, received no recognition for their work from the superintendent. Raises seemed to be apportioned on an arbitrary or uniform basis, without reference to the quality of work of the individual. In short, for any number of reasons, the greater part of the meaningfulness and satisfaction of their work had disappeared for these people.

Yet this same group waxed enthusiastic when they talked about their children and, more especially, their children's participation in team and individual sports. Although I have no statistics to back up such a generalization, I would venture that there is a strong tie between job dissatisfaction, on the one hand, and a disproportionate concern with offspring's success in sports, on the other. Children thus became the symbols or carriers of their parents' frustrated competitiveness in the work place. The parent can take pride in the child's success or blame the coach for his or her failure. In any case, the parent soon vicariously invests more of a commitment in the child's athletic life than in his or her own work life. And, as job dissatisfaction now arises earlier in professional careers, compensatory interest in children's participation in sports often arises when the children are very young.

Not surprisingly, however, the intensity of the parents' interest, and the "freighted" or vicarious nature of it, weighs on the child and robs the sporting activity of its playfulness and pleasure. The well-known sports writer John Underwood recently produced a telling indictment of the Little Leagues—the worst destroyers of the playfulness of sport.

> *The sine qua non of sport is enjoyment. When you take that away, it's no longer sport. Perhaps the worst creators of specialists are the Little Leagues in all sports. Although some observers believe there's much value in them, the Leagues have their own ethics. "Abolish the Little Leagues," says philosopher Robert Weiss. "Forbid 'em," says sociologist David Reisman.*

> *Sports psychologist Bruce Ogelvie laments the sickening arrogance of Little League coaches, too many of whom are*

unqualified. Some coaches, says another psychologist, Thomas Tatlio, even "think sports is war." They make eight year olds sit on the bench while others play, learning nothing beyond the elitism of win-at-all-costs sport. Token participation—an inning in right field, a couple of minutes in the fourth quarter—can be equally demoralizing.

To visit on small heads the pressure to win, the pressure to be "just like mean Joe Green" is indecent. To dress children up like pros in costly outfits is ridiculous. In so doing, we take away many of the qualities that competitive sports are designed to give to the growing process.[10]

Generally it is parent need, not a child's authentic wish, that pushes children into team sports at an early age. School-age children need the opportunity to play their own games, make up their own rules, abide by their own timetable. Adult intervention interferes with the crucial learning that takes place when children arrange their own games. Certainly children learn something from competitive sports—for example, competence, self-assurance, teamwork. But this is by no means true for all or even most children who participate, many of whom end up feeling like failures.

Moreover, when job dissatisfaction pushes parents to push children to athletic success, it often extends beyond team sports. At one time, parents taught infants to swim because it was assumed they did it naturally. Today, however, on ski slopes all over the country, one can see toddlers only just over the hurdle of walking suited up like miniature spacemen in expensive ski apparel, waiting for the lift to take them to the top. These children vacation with their parents in chic ski lodges, go up and down the slopes, and participate and are treated in nearly every way as adults. Except that they aren't adults, they're children, in many cases barely beyond infancy.

It is true that children who learn a sport like skiing when they are very young may become much more physically proficient when they are adults, just as it is true that matriculation at a fine preschool may prepare the child for admission to a good secondary school and college, but only to a point. Is it really necessary to have preschoolers on the slopes? Is it in the child's best interests? Does it take into account all that we know about the specialness of the identity of children and their developmental needs?

Introducing preschool children to sports like skiing is in part symbolic. The small child waddling about in ski boots that take up a third of his or her total height is making a statement for his parents. The statement is one not only of conspicuous consumption but also of conspicious concern: "How concerned we are that our child get a head start, that he be the best." But the child is really the receptacle of his or her parents' need to escape stress by bolstering their self-esteem with a precocious son or daughter.

Likewise, parents hurry children when they insist that they acquire academic skills, like reading, at an early age. Indeed, some programs now promise parents that they can teach their children to read as infants and toddlers. The desire of parents to have their children read early is a good example of parental pressure to have children grow up fast generally. This pressure reflects parental need, not the child's need or inclination. In the second half of the book we will examine this parental need in more detail. Here we need to look at the evidence that shows that children who are being pushed to read early are indeed being urged to grow up fast. It is certainly true that some children gravitate to reading early, seeking out books and adults to read to them. Such children seem to learn to read on their own with little fuss or bother. But such children are in the minority. Studies by my colleagues and me, and by other investigators, find that only 1 to 3 children in 100 read proficiently (at the second grade level) on entrance to kindergarten. If learning to read was as easy as learning to talk, as some writers claim, many more children would learn to read on their own. The fact that they do not, despite their being surrounded by print, suggests that learning to read is not a spontaneous or simple skill.

The majority of children can, however, learn to read with ease if they are not hurried into it. Our youngest son Rick is a case in point. He is the youngest of three boys and is very outgoing, social, and verbal. He was telling full-length stories at the age of three. He is one of those youngsters who, when you ask him a question, gives you a full and richly detailed answer. Because of his verbal skills I thought he might want to learn to read at the age of four. We read a lot of books together and I asked him if he wanted to learn to read or try reading the book on his own. He did not. At least one reason, I think, was that I would no longer need to read to him and we would lose that time together.

Because my wife went back to school, we placed Rick in a very fine private school where, by the way, there was no pressure for him to read early. In fact, he would sit under the table and do math problems when the other children were reading. The teacher allowed him to work at arithmetic and didn't press the reading. In second grade, Rick became interested in reading and began bringing books home from school. Now, as a teenager, he reads for recreation as well as for school and really enjoys books. I am not sure that this would have been the case had he been forced into reading.

Studies of children who have been introduced to reading later rather than earlier support our experience with Rick. Carleton Washburn, the famed educator, conducted an elaborate study in the 1930s with children in the public schools of Winnetka, Illinois. He compared classes of children who were introduced to formal reading instruction in first grade with those who were first introduced to it in second grade. Although the children who started earlier had an initial advantage on the reading tests used to assess pupil progress, this advantage disappeared by the time the children were in grade four.

Perhaps the most interesting and intriguing part of the study was a long-term follow-up that was made when the subjects of the study were young adolescents and were attending junior high school. Observers who did not know which children had been in which group were introduced into the classrooms; they were to look at all facets of the young people's reading behavior. The observers found that the adolescents who were introduced to reading late were more enthusiastic, spontaneous readers than were those who were introduced to reading early.[11]

These data are also supported by educational information from other countries. In England, studies comparing children who attended informal (late reading) elementary schools and those who attended the formal (early reading) elementary schools reported similar findings. In Russia, formal education and instruction do not begin until children are age seven, and yet Russian children seem far from being intellectually handicapped. Early reading, then, is not essential for becoming an avid reader nor is it indicative of who will become successful professionals.

Other studies suggest that children confronted with the task of learning to read before they have the requisite mental abilities can develop long-term learning difficulties. In one high school, for example, we compared the grades of pupils who had fall birthdays (in September, October, November, and December) and had entered school before they were five with those whose birthdays were in April, May, June, and July and who entered school after they were five. For boys in particular, there was, on the average, an advantage in terms of school grades to entering kindergarten after attaining age five rather than before attaining that age.

Finally, a recent study of children who have been held back or who repeated kindergarten found that almost all of the parents involved in this practice were pleased with the result. They felt that it had given their children, who were socially or intellectually below the norm at that time, a chance to catch up at their own speed. Many of the children were able to join their own age group later. Far from being handicapped by their late introduction to basics, these children were advantaged by the opportunity to move at their own pace.[12]

If there are benefits to a gradual introduction to reading, are there costs paid by those who are trained to read early? To be sure, it depends upon the child. A child who has learned to read because he or she wanted to pays no serious penalty in school. We found, however, that most early readers do not identify themselves, perhaps for fear of being considered difficult or different. To some teachers, children who read early are a kind of threat, either because they have to do something special for them, or because they feel that someone else has usurped their prerogative to teach the child to read. A teacher of this sort—fortunately there are not many—could display a negative attitude toward an early reading child that might make the child's life in the classroom difficult.

I once encountered a more serious example of the dangers of hurrying children into reading at a school in Chicago where a very energetic teacher was training four-year-old and five-year-old black children to read. To accomplish this, the children spent long hours doing drills and exercises. There was little time in their school day for much else. I must say that when I sat with individual children and had them read to me, I was impressed at the ease and fluency with which they read the storybooks. What also impressed me was the quietness of their voices.

When I visited a first-grade group who had been through that kindergarten program, they showed the benefits in terms of reading progress. But when I had the children read to me individually, the quietness of their voices was extraordinary. They were not reading aloud but whispering so that I had to strain to hear. Although they had learned a skill, it had been at great cost, and I interpreted their low voices as a sign of embarrassment and fear. They experienced no pleasure in reading aloud or in my praise or approval of what they were doing. It almost seemed that reading had been foisted upon them, at great cost in time and effort, without their having any real understanding of the value of what they were learning. They showed the apathy and withdrawal that are frequent among children who are pushed too hard academically. (This topic will be explored more fully in the next chapter).

In this connection it is necessary to say something about television programs such as "Sesame Street" and "Electric Company." These programs, and other educational programs for children, allow young people to become acquainted with letters and sounds and numbers. But in our own studies, and in those of others, we have found that what is crucial to beginning to read is the child's attachment to an adult who spends time reading to or with the child. The motivation for reading, which is a difficult task, is social. Without that social attachment and motivation, what children see on "Sesame Street" becomes more entertainment than education. And current reading achievement scores give little evidence that such television programs have had any large-scale or long-term effects on this generation's reading achievement.

Parental pressure to hurry children academically in the early years can also be seen as a downward extension of the parental concern expressed with adolescents. "Ability grouping," for example, has been fought for decades. Parents whose teenagers operate at a slower pace than the norm insist that these young people be expected to do the same work as their faster-moving peers so that they will not fall behind. The failure of some parents to recognize the limits of their children's abilities at the high-school level has its counterpart in the insistence by some parents that their children be taught to read early. In both cases, parents seem to want their children to grow up faster than what seems reasonable for the children in question. Children should be challenged intellectually, but the challenge should be constructive, not debilitating. Forcing a child to read early, no less than forcing an adolescent to take algebra when simple arithmetic is still a problem, can be a devastating experience for a young person who is not prepared intellectually for the task. A young man of seven who was struggling with reading told me, "I can't read, I guess I'm a flop in life."

THE CHILD AS STATUS SYMBOL

Another prevalent form of stress encountered by today's parent, particularly the mother, is role conflict. Within the short space of fifteen years, the role of the middle-class woman has been profoundly altered. In the fifties, a woman who worked was looked down upon as someone who did not "care enough" to look after her husband and children. Today, however, after a decade and a half of the feminist revolution, a middle-class woman who chooses the life of the housewife is often regarded as unambitious (and therefore less intelligent then her working counterparts) and generally lacking in self-respect and female pride. The situation is complicated by the fact that with the higher divorce rate, more and more women have to work.

Thus many women are caught in a conflict between their desires to perform well the traditional role of mother (and wife) and what may well be an equally strong inclination to embrace the new professional and social possibilities that have fortunately opened up for women in our society.

Women who choose to stay at home may thus come under considerable (not necessarily entirely conscious) stress for having opted for this traditional role. In her book *The Cinderella Syndrome*, Colette Dowling captures well the emptiness and restlessness of some of these women. Despite a certain pride in their husbands' positions and income, many women "admitted to a certain eventlessness in their days. They couldn't quite break off from their bridge groups, though they described them as boring. In the empty house, when they weren't shopping or entertaining or chauffeuring the kids, they read romances."[13]

Such women are stressed, whether they realize it or not. It is likely that bridge and romance novels are escapes from reflecting about what they might really want to do with their lives. For some mothers in this situation, children serve as the only, or major, justification of an otherwise somewhat empty and boring existence: "If my children can bring me attention and respect, then I don't have to feel so bad about staying home." Unfortunately, this rationale overlooks the fact that children, under these circumstances, are all too often not permitted to be just children but are pushed to be mini-achievers. While parents have traditionally taken pride in their offspring's achievements and have been concerned about their education, it is a unique characteristic of contemporary society that we burden preschoolers with the expectations and anxieties normally (if wrongly) visited upon high school seniors. Today, parents brag not only about the colleges and prep schools their children are enrolled in but also about which private kindergartens they attend. Helen LaCroix, director of admissions at Chicago's Frances W. Parker School, has said that "it's become a little more difficult to get into a private kindergarten than to enroll in college."[14]

Parents wish, and with good reason, to have their children win admission to the classy preschools that provide not only superior education but, more importantly, facilitate entry into the "better" prep schools and colleges. However, parents (and children) too easily become trapped in the fallacious inference expressed by Darla Poythress of Atlanta's Trinity School: "Parents believe if they don't get their kids in [on the Ivy League track] at the kindergarten, they won't get them in at all."[15] Yet there is no evidence that gaining a child admission into a fine kindergarten has any real bearing on prep school or college admission. Moreover the cost of matriculation at any fine private college is escalating at such a rate that many parents may not be able to afford to enroll their children, particularly not after putting them through expensive preschools and grade schools.

The anxiety generated by the school admissions sweepstakes has a symbolic significance. "Look at us," it says, "how concerned and committed we are as parents to be doing all this for our children." Hauling the kids to school and back, attending PTA meetings and school events now become the full-time "occupation" of a young mother who feels justified in not getting a job.

Certainly, women should have the option to stay home if they wish to and be able to do so without any social stigma. Ideally, this will occur when the gains of the women's movement have been more firmly consolidated than is yet the case. The fact remains that for the present and the foreseeable future, many young mothers are stressed by their conflicting desires to stay home and to become "liberated" and take a job. For mothers who cleave to the housewife role, it is often tempting to invoke the children—and their precocious adacemic accomplishments—as the justification for their not working. In doing so, however, mothers—and fathers—are placing too heavy a burden on their children.

THE CHILD AS PARTNER

What about the mother who opts for a career *and* a family? The number of working mothers in the United States has increased substantially in the last few decades. In 1948, only 26 percent of married women with children of ages six to sixteen were engaged in, or seeking, work. Today, the percentage has doubled. The majority (51 percent) of mothers of school-age children now work. The figures for working mothers of younger children are equally impressive: one-third of the mothers of young children now work full-time or part-time outside the home (three times more than in 1948).

For many women, work is a gratifying and fulfilling experience, and many find that if they cannot "have it all," as Betty Freidan said they should, they still can have the best of the work and wife-mother roles. Nevertheless, judging by the outpouring of books and magazines articles recounting the tribulations of working mothers ("Are You Jealous of the Other Woman in Your Baby's Life?," "How Working Mothers Work It Out," "You, Too, Can Cope with Added Stress"), many women are finding work stressful.

Working women are less likely to have extended family networks to rely upon for child care and are more likely to be as concerned with the intellectual stimulation their children are receiving as with their physical care and protection. Finding quality child-care workers and facilities, particularly for infants and young children, is a constant effort and a constant stress.

In addition, women, far more than men, carry the dual burden of professional work *and* housework. A recent study showed that in 1965 men averaged about 9 hours a week doing household chores and caring for children. Ten years later, men were spending 9.7 hours a week in such activities. Women, in contrast, spent 28.8 hours per week in housekeeping and child-care activities in 1965, and 24.9 hours per week in 1975. The decrease probably reflects the fact that more women were working professionally and therefore had less time to spend at home.

Working parents, particularly mothers, are of necessity more stressed by time constraints than are nonworking parents. In such families, the children have to adjust to parental schedules rather than the reverse, as is usually the case with the nonworking mother. The children must be awakened early, dressed, fed, and taken to a caretaker, day-care center, or nursery school. Arranging car pools is time-consuming, as is picking up children and dropping them off. (And there are always those irresponsible parents who are habitually late, forget the schedule, fail to show up, and so forth).

Young children have limited powers of adaptation which are sometimes exceeded by the pressures of adult scheduling. I recall one situation in which a mother wanted to have her daughter attend a prestigious nursery school in the morning and a day-care center in the afternoon. The child became increasingly upset, and after we discussed the matter, the teacher encouraged the mother to place the child in the day-care center full-time (the school was only half-day) because the stress of transition and readaptation was too much for the young girl to tolerate.

Although the programmatic hurrying of young middle-class children appears new, it is in fact a downward extension of a kind of hurrying that has been going on for a long time at older age levels. At the elementary school level, for example, it is not unusual for some children to go to hockey practice, or swimming, or gymnastics training before school. After school these same students may take music lessons or participate in a church or civic social organization activity, such as putting on a play. The heavily scheduled preschool child of today is a downward extension of the heavily programmed elementary schoolchild. In a real sense we are hurrying young children to be hurried like older children.

Older children in homes with working parents, in turn, must learn at an early age to fend for themselves. They learn to get up on their own, choose their own clothing, make their own breakfasts, clean up after themselves, and get to school on time. Now surely these are reasonable demands to make on children and do not, *ipso facto*, constitute hurrying; it may even be said that many children in two-parent homes with only one working parent would benefit from being expected to do more for themselves.

Demands and expectations can quickly get out of hand, however. A young patient of mine illustrates the hurrying that arises when parents overburden children in this fashion. The father of the boy owned a motel and the mother was the cook in the small restaurant associated with the motel. Their son usually took out the trash and occasionally helped the chambermaids with making the beds. On Saturdays, when he wanted to play with his friends, the boy's father insisted that he work at the motel—to flatten the cans that had accumulated in a week of refuse so that the price of trash removal would be lower.

This young man (age fourteen), like most children of working parents, appreciated the economic circumstances that required him to pitch in. It was only when the demands on him became unreasonable—far out of proportion to what the parents needed their son to do—that the boy could be said to be the victim of hurrying in the sense that he was burdened with adult responsibilities and expectations too early. Only then did he begin to show signs of emotional stress.

It is not always easy for working parents to separate what is reasonable from what is not. If a child can start dinner, then why not have him or her prepare the whole meal? If the child can keep one room tidy, why not the whole house? The temptation to pile heavy domestic burdens on the child is strong for parents under stress. Helping parents is one thing; taking over their jobs and responsibilities is another.

Another way parents treat children as partners is to allow them to become decision makers. It is one thing for young children to decide what they want for dinner but is another when youngsters are expected to decide with which parent they will spend Christmas, Easter, or Passover. Decision making is hard for anyone, but it is particularly hard when it is done alone—that is, when one is a single parent—without benefit of counsel and shared responsibility. There is stress in the choosing and stress in the anticipation of consequences. "What if I quit my job?" or "What if I tell my former husband to leave the children alone?" It is natural to wish to talk such matters over with someone, but children, especially young ones, lack the experience and intellectual maturity to be of much help. Children who are placed in this uncomfortable situation recognize that they are being asked to share responsibilities for which they are unprepared, and they may resent it.

THE CHILD AS THERAPIST

Separation and divorce, perhaps the most pervasive and endemic source of stress in America today, affect one in three marriages. Thus, almost half of American children under eighteen are likely to live in single-parent homes. Though stressful to both parents (as to children), divorce and separation mean something different for men and women.

For women, the stress of a marriage in trouble or ended (by death or divorce) is compounded by the fact that many women are not prepared to survive economically. The National Advisory Council on Women's Programs report on "Neglected Women" points out that one in three American women lacks the basic skills needed to earn a reasonable living. They are "products of past educational and social patterns which do not apply to today's society."

When a woman finds herself alone and responsible for a family, her initial reaction may be one of shock and panic. For one thing, having custody of the children, the woman now feels she must fill the role of both mother and father, and solo parenting is made more difficult because there is no one to share the load with or lean upon in time of stress. One mother who put her children in day-care told me, "If I didn't get out of the house for a while, I would go crazy."

There are other stresses as well: a woman's concern about whether she is still attractive to men, or how to go about meeting men; her anxiety that she may have to spend the rest of her life single, which is to say entirely alone once the children are grown. Continued association with old friends (especially couples) from one's married days often proves more difficult for the single woman than for her bachelor ex-husband. New friends can be made, of course, but they are usually other single, divorced, or widowed women who may be under so much stress themselves that they have little support to give to others. Going to a movie or play or concert suddenly looms as a problem if the woman is not in the habit of going alone (or simply doesn't want to). In sum, needing to support children financially and emotionally, without yourself enjoying those kinds of support, is perhaps the most severe stress encountered by a female in our society.

Not surprisingly, therefore, single-women parents are developing the familiar pattern of egocentrism and hurrying that is characteristic of parents under stress. One common way that single mothers hurry their children to grow up is to treat them as confidants. In some ways this is a natural phenomenon: a young mother, living alone, begins to confide in her eight-year-old daughter. The mother may tell the girl about the "crazy" man at work who always walks around talking under his breath, or she may express some of her frustrations about co-workers or office tribulations. Such ventings may lead to anxious mutterings about the state of family finances, and then, in turn, to reports of her feelings about the men she may be dating. When a mother meets a man she is interested in, the daughter learns about him, meets him, and is perhaps asked to venture an opinion about him and/or about her mother's relationship with him.

The child in such circumstances is asked to meet a parental need in much the same way as when children are hurried into school or sports. In this instance, children are hurried into mature interpersonal relations because the parent is under stress and needs a symbolic confidant. We say "symbolic" because, of course, at eight or ten years of age, the child lacks the experience and intellectual and emotional security to be of much practical use to the mother. Rather, the child serves as sympathetic listener, which is, indeed, part of what the mother needs. Unfortunately, though, it is by no means clear that this is what the child needs. As five-year-old Deana told me, "I like Mommy's friend who smells nice but I don't like the furry one who smells bad," then wistfully, "sometimes I wish she wouldn't ask me."

Single fathers also use children as confidants. Usually they do not have custody and so realize, often for the first time, how much they not only miss but literally need their children. The man's self-esteem, like the woman's, may be at a low point as a result of separation or divorce, and he may be feeling sorry for himself. When he sees the children on weekends he may complain to them about how much money he has to give to their mother and how little this leaves him to live on. Or he may express his resentment about the arguments that caused the break-up, or his jealousy over their mother's new relationships. The children are caught in the middle of these adult conflicts. Treated as confidants whom father wants as allies, they are still expected to remain impartial (and devoted) to mother.

Many single fathers also present their children with a new romantic attachment too soon after a separation. Sometimes the father leaves the family to be with another woman, a situation that happens less often with the mother. The simple act of daddy leaving home is already an enormous shock to children. To be confronted with another woman at the same time is confusing (particularly to younger children) and challenges their implicit assumption that family relationships are binding. If the mother-father relationship can be changed so abruptly, cannot the parent-child relationship undergo the same trauma?

Single fathers who fail to visit their offspring or who fail to contribute financially to their children's upbringing stress youngsters in a different way. Despite the mother's frequent efforts to present the father in the best possible light, the children feel rejected. They are thus confronted early with the fear of abandonment. They have to grow up fast to cope with those fears.

THE CHILD AS CONSCIENCE

Not unusually, parents, in their search for symbolical relief from stress, cast the child in the role of moral arbiter. While this may happen in complete families, it is more common in single-parent homes. This phenomenon is well illustrated by two case histories taken from my clinical practice.

Alice Knoepfel (not her real name) was an attractive divorcee of age thirty-six who had two teenage children, a boy and a girl. The family lived in a large home in an upper middle-class suburb. Soon after the divorce was final, the mother began dating a man of questionable reputation and business connections who was the opposite of her staid, professional husband. Alice became pregnant. Her lover insisted that she undergo an abortion, but she refused and had the baby. Alice did not explain her pregnancy to her children; she simply expected them to accept the situation. In fact she expected more—she expected them to condone her behavior, to give it explicit moral sanction. In time her teenage son moved in with his father, and her daughter got pregnant, had an abortion, dropped out of school, and moved in with her boyfriend.

In another case, Harry Tartakower (not his real name), a forty-two-year-old mathematics professor, deserted his wife and two children (ages five and nine) for a graduate student with whom he had fallen in love. Soon after moving into the home of his new girlfriend,

Harry invited his two children to come see him. He made it clear that he expected them to accept his new living arrangement. He and his girlfriend were affectionate in front of the children and did not conceal the fact that they were sleeping together. The children were unprepared for this dramatic shift in their father's behavior and could hardly believe his attentions to a woman other than their mother. They were in a state of shock when they returned home, and only through counselling were they were able to express the anger and frustration they felt toward their father.

Both Alice and Harry tried to treat their children as adults so as to derive from them moral approbation for actions that they knew the community did not approve of. In these instances, children were thus asked to serve as symbols for the larger moral society—despite the fact that they neither fully understood nor especially approved of what their mother or father had done. By expecting children to comprehend and condone behavior that most adult members of the same society frown upon, Alice and Harry not only hurried their off-spring to grow up but also placed them under an impossible psychological burden of conflict.

The children, moreover, feel the burden and resent it. As one seven-year-old told me, speaking about his recently divorced parents, "My dad tells me things about my mom and wants me to like him more than her. And my mom tells me things about my dad and she wants me to like her more than him. They get mad if I say anything good about the other one. I get tired of being asked which one I love the most. After a while you get used to it and don't say anything."

All of us today are under a great deal of stress from our rapidly changing society. Some parents are so stressed that they become egocentric and either forget or find it impossible to use the knowledge we have about the nature and needs of children. Such parents need the support, the companionship, and the symbolic achievements of their children to relieve their stress. And the expectation that children make moral judgments and evaluations, lend a comforting ear, and make decisions is not always or necessarily harmful. Indeed, young people need to learn to make judgments and decisions. The question is not whether children should be asked to make judgments and decisions and listen attentively but rather the *appropriateness* of the particular demand given the child's age, intelligence, and level of maturity. Asking a child to decide between two fast-food restaurants is probably a good idea; requiring a child to alleviate a parental burden by selecting one of two nursery schools is unfair. By making such demands parents relieve some of the stress on themselves by stressing their children.

Chapter 3

The Dynamics of Hurrying: Schools

Many schools today reflect the contemporary bias toward having children grow up fast. In a way this has happened because our schools have become increasingly industrialized and product-oriented. Teachers are unionized, textbooks are standardized on a national level, and testing has become mechanized (machine scored) and more pervasive as a consequence. Even the elementary school day is now organized into "Carnegie" units—45 to 50 minutes a day for each subject every week. And teachers these days are held accountable for children's competencies as demonstrated on standardized tests.

The industrialization of the school is not surprising, for universal schooling in America was introduced, in part, to prepare children for new ways of living and working that were a consequence of industrialization. What is surprising about our schools today is that they have reached full industrialization just at a time when factory work, as it was once known, is becoming as obsolete as the farmer with a horse-pulled plow.

Our schools, then, are out of synch with the larger society and represent our past rather than our future. While schools are always (and necessarily) behind the times because they transmit accumulated knowledge and skills, the discrepancy is particularly great today because of the knowledge explosion and the technological revolutions that occur with machine-gun rapidity. Children do poorly in school today, in part at least, because they sense the lag between what and how they are learning in school and what is happening in the rest of the world.

Schools, in ostrichlike fashion, are responding to the challenge of poor school performance by regression. "Back to basics." Back to old methods and old materials. Back to a factory emphasis on worker (teacher) productivity and quality control (pupil competency) that is at odds with the major thrust of modern industry. What the traditional factory ignored and what modern industry recognizes is that the worker is not a robot, that he or she needs motivation, challenge, a sense of involvement, recognition, and some input in the system. Modern industry looks at the worker as a person, while schools, particularly those that use teacher-proof curricula, do not.

Schools today hurry children because administrators are under stress to produce better products. This blinds them to what we know about children and leads them to treat children like empty bottles on an assembly line getting a little fuller at each grade level. When the bottles don't get full enough, management puts pressure on the operator (the teacher, who is now held accountable for filling his or her share of the bottles) and on quality control (making sure the information is valid and that the bottle is not defective). This factory emphasis hurries children because it ignores individual differences in mental abilities and learning rates. The child who cannot keep up in this system, even if only temporarily, is often regarded as a defective vessel and is labeled learning disabled or minimally brain damaged or hyperactive. Yet these same children can easily demonstrate how much knowledge they acquire from television and how quickly they can acquire the skills needed to operate electronic games. The factory system, as we shall see in more detail later in this chapter, hurries children by ignoring individual differences and by prematurely labeling many children defective.

Much of this hurrying is accomplished with the aid of standardized tests, but schools hurry children in other ways as well. The rigid age grouping of our schools, in which all curriculum and teaching are tightly sequenced, is easily abused when administrators are under stress. When school is looked upon as an assembly line, and children as empty vessels to be filled, there is a temptation to speed up the assembly line, to increase production. Why not put in as much at kindergarten as at first grade? Why not teach fourth-grade math at grade two? Indeed, as one professor mused, why not teach philosophy at grade three? The pressure to teach subject matter at ever earlier ages will be illustrated in this chapter by what has happened with sex education. But it could equally well be demonstrated with subjects such as values clarification or social problem solving.

A final illustration of how schools hurry children is the fact that so many writers and educators today urge parents to create schools in the home. Whereas schools are concerned with children's acquisition of knowledge and with their attainment of skills, schools in the home have a different objective. Advocates of this sort of schooling are concerned with making children brighter by early intellectual stimulation. Such programs advocate hurrying children into academic subjects early, with the hopes of increasing their intelligence. This type of academic hurrying will also be discussed in full later in the chapter.

ASSEMBLY LINE LEARNING

The standardized, machine-scored test that we are so familiar with today is a relatively recent invention. Standardized tests were first introduced around the turn of the century by French psychologist Alfred Binet and his colleague Henri Simon. Binet had been commissioned by the French government to find a way to identify mentally retarded children at an early age so that they could be placed in special institutions. To develop his test, Binet went to teachers and asked them to describe the sorts of skills they had observed in children at different ages. On the basis of these teacher comments Binet constructed his test items, which dealt with language, understanding, reasoning, and motor skill.[1]

Binet standardized his "scale" by testing the items on large numbers of normal children. Any item that was passed by about 75 percent of a particular age group was assigned to that age level. If everyone at a particular age level passed the item, it was considered to be too easy for that age group. And if only half or fewer of the pupils passed the item, it was considered to be too difficult. This manner of assigning items to a particular age (and later grade) level results in what has come to be known as a "norm-referenced" test. A child's performance on such a test is always interpreted with respect to a norm group.

Binet assigned six tests to each age level from age two to adult (after age sixteen no further age discriminations were made). A child's score was reported not in points but in terms of what Binet called Mental Age; two months credit was given for each test a child passed. The child's total score was the total number of months of credit he or she attained; expressed in years and months, this total month score constituted the child's Mental Age. Hence a child who received sixty months of credit would have a Mental Age of five, regardless of his or her chronological age.

Binet insisted upon the Mental Age concept because he wanted to keep the measurement of intelligence in psychological units. He was very wary of using numbers to describe intelligence and did not approve of the Intelligence Quotient (IQ) concept introduced by William Stern. The IQ concept proposed a measure of "relative brightness," how bright children were vis-à-vis their age mates, rather than just an absolute measure of brightness such as the Mental Age. The Intelligence Quotient was defined as IQ = Mental Age (MA) ÷ Chronological Age (CA) × 100. A child with a Mental Age of 60 months and a chronological age of 60 months would thus have an IQ of 100. A child whose MA was greater than his or her CA would have an IQ of more than a hundred; a child with a CA greater than his or her MA would have an IQ of less than 100.

Intelligence tests were useful in screening retarded children but Binet was very much aware of their dangers and wrote: "We should at least spare from this mark [a test score that would send a child to an institution for the retarded] those who do not deserve it. Mistakes are excusable, especially at the beginning. But if they become too gross we can injure the name of these institutions."[2] Not to mention the costs to the children involved. Unfortunately, Binet's hope was not realized, and as we shall see, we are still making mistakes with tests.

During the First World War a new innovation in testing was introduced: the group test. A group-administered test, the Army Alpha, was used to screen recruits who were not bright enough to be soldiers. (One finding was that the average recruit had, according to the test norms, a Mental Age of thirteen.) The introduction of group intelligence tests led the way to the proliferation of group tests of vocational aptitude, personality, and school achievement.

The next technological innovation in testing was the introduction of machine-scored tests. Specifically, the IBM score sheet, which could be electronically read and scored, had momentous implications for schools. Once machines took over the drudgery of scoring tests, the way was open for their extensive use in the schools, as well as in industry. There are few innovations in education that have had any staying power, but the machine-scored test is the exception and has become a major force in contemporary education.

Indeed, machine-scored group testing, probably more than any other single influence, has heightened the factory quality of our schools, pushing them to turn out uniform products. This emphasis has grown dramatically over the last ten years as dissatisfaction with the schools and with children's attainments has become more pronounced on the part of both parents and legislators. Whether blame is placed on television, single-parent homes, mothers working, or the decline of authority, children's academic performance is declining, and the efforts currently under way to remedy the situation rely heavily on testing and teacher accountability. This has stirred what could be the great debate of the early eighties. Whereas everyone agrees that children should learn some basic skills, there is great debate over whether factory management or child-centered approaches will have the most effect. The problem with the factory management system is that it pushes children too much and puts them into a uniform mold. The child-centered systems, in contrast, may not push children enough.

For the moment, the factory management systems in education seem to be the most prevalent, and consequently children are being pressured to produce for the sake of teachers and administrators. The following examples from various programs around the country will show the kinds of testing and curriculum pressure many children are under today. Of course, children need to learn the basics, but we need to consider the costs of whatever approach we employ in teaching them.

New Jersey provides a good example of the controversy over the factory management of schools. About five years ago New Jersey instituted a Testing Program called the MBS (Minimum Basic Skills) that assessed reading and math skills. Teachers were held accountable for the performance of their pupils, and remarkable improvement in test scores was made from 1979 to 1980. Education writer Fred Hechinger quoted Commissioner Fred Burke in the *New York Times:* "The improvement in those areas were not the result of any magic program or any singular teaching strategy, they were . . . simply proof that accountability is crucial and that, in the past five years, it has paid off in New Jersey."

But not everyone agrees with Commissioner Burke. William Shine (superintendent of schools in Cherry Hill, New Jersey) and Norman Goldman (director of instruction, New Jersey Education Association, Trenton district) write: "To a superintendent whose district is in danger of failing it, the minimum competency test would certainly become a major curriculum imperative. Teachers, reluctant to risk their futures, might also emphasize passing the test as the number one goal of their classes. If teachers' and administrators' jobs and reputations depend on their students test scores, then it is easy to predict where they will focus their time and energy."[3]

And further: "Anyone trained in education knows there is a difference between skills and the ability to use those skills. When skills are learned in isolation the connection between them and their use is tenuous. Creative teachers prefer to employ various instructional techniques so that children can integrate subject matter into their lives. Educational theorists have long held that repetitive drill in basic skills not connected to comprehension or composition is the least efficient way to educate and in some instances is even counterproductive."[4]

To this attack Commissioner Burke responded: "This year MBS test results are not distorted. They reflect a true rise in minimum basic skills achievement by students, statewide. Test score increases in the basic skills have been observed in other standardized tests, not just in the MBS tests. This reinforces the state's belief that students are making real progress in basic skills.

"There also is no evidence to suggest that teachers are 'teaching to the test.' To imply this is to say that teachers are not doing their job. We believe that legislators, teachers, administrators, board members, parents and students worked hard to improve basic skills performance because they recognize the serious consequences to themselves and to education if they do not."[5]

The last paragraph highlights the pressure issue. Aside from the merits or lack of merit of the MBS program, the result is that children are pressured to achieve early. It is not clear that learning the limited skills required by tests is the best way for children to master the basic skills. As Jean Dresden Grambs says: "The full impact of mechanized testing has yet to be assessed. Instruction geared to the right answer out of four 'possibles' is instruction that cannot develop depth of conceptualization or provide time for the meanderings of inquiry. Expository writing is eliminated and S.A.T. scores of course go down. Sale of duplicating paper for short answer tests is rising while the sale of lined composition paper is down."[6]

And Kenneth Keniston says: "We measure the success of schools not by the kinds of human beings they promote but by whatever increases in reading scores they chalk up. We have allowed quantitative standards, so central to the adult economic system, to become the principle yardstick for our definition of our children's worth."[7]

Thus Grambs and Keniston suggest that the narrow focus produced by mass testing is detrimental to good education. Learning to read, for example, accompanies learning to write, listen, and clearly articulate ideas. Even teachers who are not teaching to the tests may be so burdened by the management demands of testing programs that there is little time to really look at children's work, to read compositions, and so on. Management systems take teachers away from teaching.

Consider the program recently instituted in Los Angeles: "The Los Angeles Unified School District, like many other districts, recently developed a K–6 continuum of essential competencies in reading, language, and mathematics and instituted a yearly survey of these essential skills at each grade level. . . . The traditional norm referenced (using the performance of a national sample to assess an individual's progress) achievement tests are rather insensitive to the effects of classroom instruction, and that grade level competency tests provide a more useful and accurate picture of a student's accomplishments."[8]

Tests are now determining school curriculum, and the conduct of teaching is beginning to look more and more like that of a factory foreman than that of a true teacher. In the system described above, for example, teachers have to keep "class progress sheets" at each grade level for each subject. "Their sheets list the skills to be assessed at that grade level and have columns to be checked when the skill is taught and when tested. They include:

- Teacher worksheets for yearly goal setting.
- Teacher worksheets for weekly scheduling.

- Forms and scales for monitoring class progress, observing instruction, and identifying and remediating instructional problems.[9]

Teachers who have to live with such systems have little time to interact with their students, grade papers, or engage in other activities essential for true learning. As Henry M. Brickell, president of Policy Studies in Education, concludes from a broad survey of educational research: "The three most important ingredients in the [school] setting are the student, the teacher, and the length of time they are together. Children have different personal characteristics (especially intelligence) which have a primary effect on how much they learn. Teachers have different personal characteristics (especially intelligence, charisma, affection for children) which have a primary effect on how well they teach. Given a particular student and a particular teacher, the *length of time they are together* influences student learning more than anything else. Once those three are established, researchers will discover little if any significant difference among various teaching methods."[10]

Management systems reduce the amount of time that the teacher and student are together; bookkeeping comes before teaching. Consider the following description of the management system recently introduced in Detroit—Measurement Driven Instruction:

> Detroit public schools have added a new dimension to student minimum competency testing—measurement driven instruction. Its purpose is not primarily to keep low performing students from receiving high school diplomas but to improve instruction in basic skills and eventually in other areas.
>
> Detroit's program stresses special features that are relevant to instruction as well as to assessment.
>
> - The program focuses on a manageable number of community endorsed competencies in reading, writing and mathematics.
> - Student mastery of basic skills is assessed by criterion referenced tests built especially to measure the competencies.

- *Instructional improvement hinges on communicating competency descriptions to Detroit's teachers, students and citizens.*[11]

There is no question that programs such as those in New Jersey, Los Angeles, and Detroit may have a beneficial effect in that they force a tightening up of loose educational practice. Programs such as Mastery Learning, instituted in the Chicago Public Schools, can break teacher stereotypes about who can and cannot learn. Michael Katims, head of Mastery Learning in Chicago, was quoted in the *Cincinnati Post* as saying: "If you demonstrate to teachers that kids can learn, it can have a shattering effect upon the classroom. Good students make good teachers more than the other way around."[12]

Management programs, accountability, and test scores are what schools are about today and children know it. They have to produce or else. This pressure may be good for many students, but it is bound to be bad for those who can't keep up. Their failure is more public and therefore more humiliating than ever before. Worse, students who fail to achieve are letting down their peers, their teacher, the principal, the superintendent, and the school board. This is a heavy burden for many children to bear and is a powerful pressure to achieve early and to grow up fast.

The effects on young people of these management approaches is the opposite of what was intended. The high-school dropout rate, which had been level for the past ten years, is on the rise again—particularly in those states, such as Connecticut, New York, and New Jersey, that have introduced management systems. At the other end of the spectrum, the emphasis on early identification of children with potential learning problems forces children to think of themselves as defective before they have had a chance to show what they can do. The introduction of remedial reading programs at first grade shows how far this mania for early identification has gone.

The pressure has had other effects as well. What schools teach children, more than anything else, is that the end result, or grade, is more important than what that grade was supposed to mean in the way of achievement. Children are much more concerned with grades than with what they know. So it isn't surprising that when these young people go out into the work world, they are less concerned with the job than with the pay and the perquisites of the job. What schools have to realize is that the attitudes they inculcate in young people are carried over into the occupational world.

Even more discouraging is the dishonesty and cheating that are fostered by the overemphasis on testing. If it is the grade you get, rather than what you know, that counts, then the most important thing is to get the highest grade. The testing scandals over the New York State Regents Exam and at our military academies are only the tip of the iceberg. Again, why should this be surprising to us (as it seems to be)? If young people are treated as products, as worth only as much as they score on a test, then they need have no moral or ethical scruples than any other industrial product would have. Treated as objects, young people can hardly be held either ethically or morally accountable.

SEX FOR BEGINNERS

Just as there is controversy over the current management emphasis in schools and its resulting pressure on children, there is also controversy over the new sex education and its impact on children. The idea of sex education is not new, of course. Around the turn of the century, G. Stanley Hall discovered, via his questionnaires, that adolescent women believed that they could become pregnant by kissing; he thus advocated sex education posthaste. In the same way, boys had many conceptions of the harm (brain rotting, early death, and so forth) that would be produced by masturbation. Early sex education was meant primarily to correct misinformation.[13]

This emphasis on correcting misinformation continued well into the 1950s when sex education—billed as "preparation for marriage and family life"—was most often part of home economics courses. By then the sex education curriculum had expanded to include information about the dangers of venereal disease and premarital pregnancy. In addition, some aspects of sexual anatomy and its functions were taught in courses on human biology. Such material, however, was reserved for junior and senior high school students.

In the 1960s, because of the social upheavals of that period and particularly in response to the women's movement, sex education began to explore some of the human aspects of sexuality. Issues such as clothing and provocative behavior, dating, peer pressure, and the personal consequences of being sexually active were discussed. Again, most of these programs were geared to students at the high school level. Such programs are probably the most frequent in our schools today except that they are now increasingly taught at the junior high level rather than at the high school level.

Still, the kind of sex education that is controversial is not the benign health education described above but a much more explicit and value-laden program that has been adopted in some schools. The new sex education programs are the product of mental health specialists—psychologists, social workers, and organizations such as Planned Parenthood. What these various groups have in common is a concern about the increasing number of teenagers who are sexually active, the alarming rise of venereal disease in the teenage population, and the ever-increasing numbers of teenage girls who become pregnant each year. The new sex educators want not only to educate and inform but also to prevent some of the negative consequences of premature sexual activity.

The new sex education programs also include material with another goal—sexual adjustment. The new programs aim to help young people feel more comfortable in expressing the many facets of their sexuality, to be more sensitive to the needs of their partners, and to enjoy their sexuality as a normal and healthy part of their lives. Because of this emphasis upon sexual adjustment, the new programs sometimes seem to be condoning, if not advocating, teenage sexuality.

The theme of the new sex education programs is conveyed by Carol Cassell, education director of Planned Parenthood, who was quoted in the *New York Times:* "My vision for the future involves happier, more sexually adjusted individuals, with a more positive feeling about themselves and others, and a reduction of sexual dysfunction in marriage."[14]

The new courses on sex education include much more than anatomy; they deal with such issues as dating behavior, abortion, contraception, homosexuality, masturbation, mental illness, and the terminal stages of disease and death. The teaching technique is usually discussion, which is often triggered by videotapes or by films such as *We Were Just Too Young,* the depressing story of a teenage couple trying to rear their two-year-old son with little money and frequent separations in a household where the father physically abuses the mother. Another film, *Who Happen To Be Gay*, depicts gay professionals living happy, productive lives.

The following excerpt, recorded by Constance Horner, will convey the flavor of some of the discussions that can occur in a sex education class:

> *It is a warm afternoon, but the 40 sixth graders, half black, half white, in a quiet school in a small middle-income community on the East Coast are paying attention.*
>
> *Hands tucked into his orange traffic patrol belt, his eyes cast down, Allen stands next to his desk, rocking back and forth, heel to toe, toe to heel. Sweat trickles down his baby fat cheeks. He doesn't know the answer. In a friendly way the teacher prods. "Come on Allen. You know what 'making out' means. Remember last week you told me what you want to do when you see those girls coming down the hall?"*
>
> *A long pause follows, and then a soft answer.*
> *"Kiss 'em."*
> *"And what else?"*
> *"Hold their hands."*
> *"And that's all, right? You didn't tell me anything about feeling them—although I've been watching your hands . . . ." The pupils giggle and the teacher relaxes. The concept has been defined. Sexual behavior must be age-appropriate. For a sixth grader that means kissing and holding hands.*[15]

Courses at the high school level are even more explicit and deal with questions such as these that were put in sex educator Peggy Buck's Sex Question Box:

> *What do you think about kids our age having sex?*
>
> *Should age be a factor in deciding whether or not to have intercourse with a partner if you have a good understanding relationship in which you can discuss birth control?*
>
> *Is it safe to have sex during a girl's period?*

How accurate are home pregnancy tests?

If you have an abortion what problems can it cause later?

Why do guys get turned on so easily?[16]

The openness of these questions by high school students is refreshing, and apparently such courses taught by able teachers to juniors and seniors in high school have value, as many of the student evaluations indicate: "When I hear my friends talking about sex they just don't know what's happening" or "a lot that people think teens know about sex, they really don't know and wouldn't even think to ask."[17]

One can certainly justify such programs, and sex educator Peggy Buck writes: "Since sexuality is at the heart of adolescent consciousness, one isolated course is only the start of a program that might help them achieve full integrity as sexual beings. As they experience their own developing sexuality, they are faced with confusing adult behaviors and values and they are manipulated by the sexploitation of virtually every advertisement they see. They are desperate for information and serious dialogue that will help them grow into sexually healthy persons. Without this opportunity, the strong ones will evolve their own codes, contemptuous of a society that simultaneously titillates and represses. Those who are less strong will remain confused. Many will slip into behavior that is harmful to themselves and others."[18]

The problem is, of course, that sex education for sixteen- or seventeen-year-olds is rarely appropriate for eleven- and twelve-year-olds. Inevitably, however, the conviction "earlier is better," which so dominates today's educational climate, means that such programs will be and are being used with preteen and young teenagers who may be given more information than they want or need. The real question is not whether sex education should be provided in the schools but, rather, whether what is offered in the name of sex education is meaningful and useful to the age groups for whom it is provided. Unfortunately, the answer is often "no," and many young people are exposed to programs and information that reflect adult anxieties about teenage sexuality much more than the very real concerns and anxieties experienced by the young people to whom the programs are directed.

There is even some question about school-based sex education for any age group. When asked whether sex information cleared up children's distorted ideas about sexuality, child therapist Bruno Bettelheim replied: "No, because correct information about sex does not do away with incorrect information. That's a prejudice. New information is just grafted onto the misinformation and leads to greater confusion. Right here in Palo Alto, a colleague's daughter came home from school and said 'We saw a movie that shows where babies come from.' Her mother asked her where babies come from and the little girl said 'Babies are brought by the nurse to the mother, I saw it in the movie.' "

Asked what good sex education might be like, Bettelheim replied: "In my opinion, sex education is impossible in the classroom. Sex education is a continuous process and it begins the moment you are born. It's in how you are bathed, how you are diapered, how you are toilet trained, in respect for the body, in the notion that bodily feelings are pleasant and that bodily functions are not disgusting. You don't learn about sex from parental nudity or by showering together. That's nonsense. How you feel about sex comes from watching how your parents live together, how they enjoy each other's company, the respect they have for each other. Not from what they do in bed to each other."[19]

And as far as classes in sex education are concerned, Bettelheim says: "I think even such classes are a danger and that they are implicated in the increase in teenage sex and teenage pregnancies. You cannot have sex education without saying that sex is natural and that most people find it pleasurable. Sex education cannot teach respect for the integrity of one's body. The problem in sex is sexual anxiety, and you cannot teach about sexual anxiety because each person has different anxieties."[20]

So, there is far from total agreement as to whether sex education in the schools is beneficial to *any* age group, much less to young people approaching adolescence. One has to conclude that sex education in the schools reflects adult anxiety about young people's sexuality. The "prejudice" that early sex education will produce children with "healthy sexuality" is open to serious question—even if experts agreed as to what healthy sexuality is—which they do not. Sex education in the schools, given at even younger ages and without clear-cut theoretical or research justification, is another way in which some contemporary schools are encouraging their pupils to grow up fast.

THE SCHOOL IN THE HOME

As mentioned in the previous chapter, parents can hurry children by pushing them into educational settings where they receive formal instruction early. Another avenue to early academic achievement is to have the parents teach their children in the home. Indeed, a number of current books are aimed at helping parents to teach their children at home in the preschool years. Books such as *Give Your Child a Superior Mind* by Engelmann and Engelmann, *Growing Wisdom, Growing Wonder* by Gregg and Knotts, *How to Raise a Brighter Child* by Joan Beck are different in philosophy but all three insist on teaching young children basic concepts and skills. *Helping Your Child Learn Right from Wrong* by Simon and Olds has a different emphasis but again puts the parent in a teaching role. Other books such as *Cushla and Her Books* or *Living with Your Hyperactive Child* are aimed at children with special needs.[21]

The contemporary interest of parents in providing schooling at home has many roots and motivations. Some parents are unhappy with the schools and feel that they can do a better job or that children need a head start if they are to succeed. Other parents (particularly women) may feel guilty about staying home and therefore teach their children as a rationalization for staying home. Parents may also see it as part of their role as parents. And others teach their children at home for status or ego reasons so that they can boast about a superior or gifted child.

Parents, of course, always teach their children. From the first baby talk to the first rattle placed in the crib, to the encouragement of walking, bowel, and bladder training, self-care, and awareness of household dangers such as poisons, electric sockets, and so on, parents teach their children a wide range of concepts and skills. Parents also teach their children manners, as well as motor skills such as riding a tricycle, wagon, or bicycle. In the ordinary course of parenting, mothers and fathers do a great deal of teaching in the many domains where children will eventually have to function independently.

Such teaching is, by and large, informal. Parents have no pre-scribed program or lesson plan, and the teaching goes on as it is needed by the situation or the child. Inasmuch as there is no proven "best way" to teach children such things as bowel or bladder con-trol or manners, parents make do with what they experienced as children and with what "feels" right to them. For the most part they succeed quite well.

But the new books go beyond this so-called informal teaching and informal curriculum. They suggest that parents engage in for-mal, or programed, instruction with their children; they advocate that parents deliberately teach their young children academic skills. The rationale is that new research has shown that the early years are ones in which children learn very rapidly and that therefore this time should not be missed. Gregg and Knotts, two parent-authors who taught their children at home, express their reasons:

> *The latest word from the experts is that what happens to a child before he gets to school is all important for his future emotional, social and intellectual development. Their message seems to be that diapers and discipline are no longer enough. This puts you as parents in a muddle if you are supposed to create security, educate, and live a little yourselves too. If learning really begins at birth, what is it children learn? Can parents help or does it just happen? We know parents can help and have their own lives too, but how do experts' findings translate to your kitchens and living rooms, your busy lives?*[22]

The "experts" whom Gregg and Knotts cite in support of their work include Jean Piaget (who believed children should not be pushed but, rather, that they be allowed to grow at their own pace, with minimal adult interference) and Maria Montessori, the famed Italian educator who believed that teaching was a very difficult and challenging profession that required highly specialized training. Montessori founded *teacher*-training, not parent-training, institutes. Neither Piaget nor Montessori ever advocated that parents teach their children in a formal way at home. Both these investigators rec-ognized the stress and pressure that went along with formal schooling and perhaps felt it best not to compound and complicate the difficult task of parenting by asking parents to be teachers too.

A somewhat different justification for home-schooling is the efficacy with which it has been done in the past. Engelmann and Engelmann, for example, cite the book *The Early Mental Traits of Three Hundred Geniuses* in which author Catharine Morris Cox recounts brief biographies of such people as Copernicus, Rousseau, Voltaire, Goethe, and John Stuart Mill. The Engelmanns cite many histories like the following:

> *Until he was 14, Mill [John Stuart Mill, English philosopher, writer, logician, and economist] was educated at home by his father. He began to learn Greek at three; and from then to his ninth year he studied Greek classics, making daily reports of his reading. At the same time, under his father's direction he read innumerable historical works.*[23]

On the basis of Cox's biographies the Engelmanns conclude: "Every single genius at the top end of the IQ scale received intensive training. Every single one was subjected to an extremely active environment, not one that folded its hands and waited for the child to 'mature' but one that went after him and trained him when he was still of preschool age."

The Engelmanns then provide the following from Mill's autobiography:

> *I have no remembrance of the time when I began to learn Greek, I have been told that it was when I was three years old. My earliest recollection on that subject is that of committing to memory what my father termed Vocables, being lists of common Greek words with their signification in English, which he wrote for me on cards. Of grammar, until some years later, I learned no more than the inflexions of the nouns and verbs, but after a course of Vocables, proceeded at once to translation; and I faintly remember going through Aesop's fables, the first Greek book I read. . . . What he (my father) was himself willing to undergo for the sake of my instruction, may be judged from the fact that I went*

through the whole process of preparing my Greek lessons in the same room and at the same table at which he was writing; and as in those days, Greek and English Lexicons were not, and I could make no more use of a Greek and Latin lexicon than could be made without having yet begun to learn Latin, I was forced to have recourse to him for the meaning of every word which I did not know. This incessant interruption, he, one of the most impatient of men, submitted to and wrote under interruption several volumes of his History and all else he had to write during those years.[24]

The Engelmanns then provide the following rationale for their program of school in the home: "From Mill's account you receive the picture of a boy—not a machine—that learned Greek at three and Latin at eight. Granted his performance is good, but notice the characteristics of the environment, evident from Mill's quote. The environment works throughout the child's waking hours; it takes pains to insure that the child has learned his lessons; it carefully reduces the possibility of mistakes; it establishes a clear pattern for using what is learned; it forces the child when necessary; it establishes firm models for him to follow. This is an environment that will succeed with *any* healthy infant. Yes, if we could play a little game with history and switch the real John Stuart Mill with some unfortunate infant from the slums of London, the history books wouldn't change very much. The unfortunate would become a Mill."[25]

It is also true that many people who did not receive instruction in their early years ended up quite successful. Consider the following three case histories:

Girl, aged sixteen, orphaned, willed to custody of grandmother by mother, who was separated from alcoholic husband, now deceased. Mother rejected homely child, who has been proven to lie and to steal sweets. Swallowed penny to attract attention at five. Father was fond of child. Child lived in fantasy as the mistress of father's household for years. Four young uncles and aunts in household cannot be managed by the grandmother, who is widowed.

*Aunt, emotional over love affair, locks self in room. Grand-
mother resolves to be more strict with granddaughter since
she fears she has failed with her own children. Dresses
granddaughter oddly. Refuses to let her have playmates,
puts her in braces to keep her back straight. Does not send
her to grade school. Aunt on paternal side of family crip-
pled, uncle asthmatic.*

*Boy, seven, secondary school, has obtained certificate from
physician stating that nervous breakdown makes it necessary for him to leave school for six months. Boy not a good
all-around student . . . has no friends . . . teachers find him a
problem . . . spoke late . . . father ashamed of son's lack of
athletic ability . . . poor adjustment to school. Boy has odd
mannerisms, makes up own religion, chants hymns by
himself. Parents regard him as "different."*

*Boy, aged six, head large at birth. Thought to have had
brain fever. Three siblings died before his birth; mother
does not agree with relatives and neighbors that child is
probably abnormal. Child sent to school, diagnosed as
mentally ill by teacher. Mother is angry. Withdraws child
from school, says she will teach him herself.*[26]

These three biographies—of Eleanor Roosevelt, Albert Einstein, and Thomas Edison—illustrate that early instruction is not essential to later high intelligence or outstanding achievement. Moreover, in a study conducted by Goertzel and Goertzel, over three-fifths of the four hundred eminent people studied expressed dissatisfaction with school and school teachers, although four-fifths showed exceptional talent. If gifted children dislike formal education at school, why should they like or need it at home? Indeed, what Goertzel and Goertzel found to be most characteristic of gifted children was that they came from "homes [where] there is a love of learning in one or both parents, often accompanied by a physical exuberance and a persistent drive toward goals. Fewer than 10 percent of parents failed to show a strong love of learning."[27]

Parents who love learning will create a stimulating environment for children, which is far more beneficial to them than specific instruction. Parents who fill the house with books, paintings and music, who have interesting friends and discussions, who are curious and ask questions provide young children with all the intellectual stimulation they need. In such an environment, formal instruction would be like ordering a hamburger at a four-star restaurant.

That there are actual dangers in home schooling (as opposed to the home enrichment described above) are illustrated by Deaken in *The Children on the Hill*. In the story, the child-rearing practices of a young couple, Maria and Martin, are described. Both Maria and Martin had bad experiences at school and decided to educate their children on their own. Their program of instruction was guided by basic principles of love, unconditional acceptance, and nonviolence. Maria's approach to education was to follow each child's lead and to nourish his or her spontaneous interests.[28]

To illustrate this approach, consider Adam, the second child. Adam happened to see a toy piano in a store and became intrigued with it. The mother bought the child the toy piano, which he proceeded to play with, almost to the exclusion of everything else. The mother continued to encourage this interest, and Adam soon had a real piano on which to explore his interest in sounds and melodies. His room was full of sheet music and little else. When he eventually went to school as an adolescent, he did not adjust well and could relate to people only in relation to the piano or to music. Adam's brother, Christian, also became narrowly specialized but in the field of mathematics and, like his brother, had difficulty relating to other people.

With these two boys, as with others like chess master Bobby Fisher, the exclusive preoccupation with a single field of interest supported by parents in early childhood can lead to superior performance in the field if the child has the native talent. But it can also lead to narrow specialization, social and vocational maladjustment, and personal unhappiness. The most productive people have a variety of interests and avocations. Indeed, major contributions are often made by individuals from *outside* the discipline of their contribution—Freud was a neurologist, Einstein was a mathematician, and Piaget was trained as a biologist. True innovation comes from broadened, not narrow, perspectives.

The problem, then, with the programs of those who advocate schooling in the home is the same found in the schools themselves. Schooling and education are thought of in narrow terms, of attaining basic concepts and skills. But education—true education—is coincident with life and is not limited to special skills or concepts and particularly not to test scores. True education does not come packaged or sequenced. Much of it is spontaneous, an outgrowth of openness and curiosity. It is this attitude toward learning, this openness to questioning and curiosity that parents need to impart to their children.

Home schooling also has another danger. While some parents can shift from parent to teacher role with ease, others cannot. When they begin teaching their young children in a formal way, many parents assume a strict demeanor which is both foreign and frightening to their children. In addition, they may assume an evaluative posture—"You have to get this right or you are stupid and a bad reflection on me"—that could hardly be beneficial to the child's sense of self.

Clearly there is much that parents can and should do to promote the intellectual development of their children, but this need not be and probably shouldn't be formal instruction. Taking the time to talk to children, to answer their questions is an important form of intellectual stimulation; reading to your child is another. Going on trips to the park, the zoo, the museum, and the country are important learning experiences for children. Young children, after all, don't know the world very well and the best education parents can provide is to acquaint them with that world through language, shared activities, and trips in the context of love and protection.

Many parents who read these pages will conclude that I am yet another advocate of permissiveness in the sense of being soft on kids; but this really is not the case. I believe in discipline, in hard work, and in learning basic skills. I do not believe that children should be left to their own devices nor that rules are made to be broken. I am opposed to schooling practices that not only will not work but that may harm children.

The competency-based instructional programs are a case in point. In the last week of June 1981, the New York City School system said it was holding back about 17 percent of all fourth graders and about 21 percent of all seventh graders (a total of about 24,745 pupils) because of reading deficiencies. This is more than double the number held back in the past. About half of the students will attend a six-week summer school program aimed at bringing them up to grade level. What will be done with the children who are held back? Are classes going to get even larger, thus placing incoming fourth graders at a disadvantage? Are fifth-grade teachers going to teach fourth grade, a curriculum they don't know? Or are children going to develop better cheating skills so they can be promoted at last?

The point is that "quick fixes" in education never work. We know what good education is. Substantial learning is taking place in many urban, suburban, and private schools that provide well-trained and committed teachers, reasonable class size, and adequate materials and support. Pressuring children to get certain marks on tests that at best measure rote knowledge is hardly the way to improve the education of our children. What good is it if children can read but not understand what they read or if they know how to compute but not where, when, or what to compute?

Our educational establishment suffers from the same ills as did our industrial establishment: it has become too product-oriented and has ignored the workers. By pressing for ever faster, more efficient production, the needs of the workers—self-esteem, pride in their work, and a sense of accomplishment—suffer. The result is shoddy workmanship, absenteeism, and lack of commitment to the job and the industry. The school's response, to push children even harder, is bound to fail.

Industry is beginning to recognize that the workers are people who have a need to participate in decision making and to learn different facets of the industry they are involved in. Companies, such as Chrysler, that are using these new approaches are finding that quality is up and absenteeism is down. If we have to see our schools as factories, then we should learn from our modern-day factory experience. Hurrying workers and threatening them do not work. Treating them as human beings who want to take pride in their work, who don't want to be confined to the same routine, and who want the opportunity to express their opinions and to have those opinions taken seriously does work.

Such an approach, in industry or schooling, is not permissive—it is democratic in the best sense of the term. Children need direction and limits, but they also need to be able to make choices that are appropriate for them to make and to take appropriate responsibilities. Democracy is the balance between total control and total freedom, and what we need in education, as in industry, is true democracy. Only when the values upon which this country was founded begin to permeate our educational and industrial plants will we begin to realize our full human and production potentials.

A closing word about dynamics: Schools and school personnel are currently under pressure to produce improved test scores of pupils. We have seen that when people are under stress they become egocentric and do not—cannot—appreciate other people's needs or interests. Hence the new "measurement-driven programs" ignore what we know about children for the same reason that parent schedules hurry children—the adults who are involved cannot put to use their knowledge about children and education. If we take some of the pressure off schools and school administrators, we will take some of the pressure off children.

Chapter 4

The Dynamics of Hurrying: The Media

Whereas education may transmit our cultural past, the media broadcast our present and project our future. Media—television, radio, newspapers, magazines, movies—extend our senses, as Marshall McLuhan has suggested.[1] Efforts by movie makers to give us the experience of three-dimensional space, stereo sound, and most recently, the appropriate smells, all attest to the efforts of media to extend our senses. The move from silent films to talkies and from black-and-white television to color is but another index of the relentless effort of media to extend our sensory experience in space and in time.

If media extend our senses, education aims at extending our memory. Schools are charged with transmitting accumulated knowledge and skills and, as such, necessarily represent our cultural past rather than our cultural future. As we have seen, despite our knowledge about children's development, schools still see children as empty bottles on an assembly line of grades—each grade fills the bottle up a little more, the bottle representing the child's memory. Schools are hurrying children by speeding up the assembly line, by trying to fill up the bottles faster but not, it should be said, by trying to get more in.

TELEVISION

Media hurry our children in quite a different way than schools; they extend senses into distant places so that we can experience what is happening all over the world. This is particularly true of television.

First of all, television extends our senses in ways that other media cannot—news is a prime example. Newspapers and films have to present news events after they happen. Radio can present events as they happen but the events are translated by the words and voice of the broadcaster. Few broadcasters are as good as Orson Welles was in his famous broadcast of "The War of the Worlds," wherein he had his listeners believing we were being attacked by Martians. Radio requires us to retranslate words into sensory images and thus stimulates the imagination.

Television, however, extends our senses immediately, without verbal mediation by a broadcaster. Indeed, with television such mediation often appears intrusive and offsetting—witness audience reactions to sports broadcaster Howard Cosell. Because television does not require verbal encoding and decoding to extend our experience, it is very accessible to children and hurries them into experiences not open to them before.

The following example will illustrate this point: Young children usually have trouble telling time from a clock face because a clock face presents them with certain logical difficulties. One place represents two different numbers and two different time units: the "three" represents both three hours after twelve *and* fifteen minutes after any hour. The child has to understand that the same place can represent different time units, and such understanding requires the concrete operations of intelligence identified by Piaget, which will be described in detail later.

But today even young children can tell time if they are given a digital clock. The digital clock makes telling time easier by removing some of the logical difficulties presented by a clock face. Whereas on a clock face different units are located in the *same* place, on a digital clock each unit has its *own* place—there is a place for hours, minutes, and seconds. There is no longer any confusion between place and unit, and the child can tell time by reading the numbers directly without having to translate from where the "big hand" and the "little hand" are located. The difference between a digital clock and a conventional clock is also the difference between television and radio.

With television, many of the conceptual and logical barriers to extending children's experiences posed by the other media are effectively swept away. Children no longer have to read or be able to translate a broadcaster's words in order to experience events that are happening simultaneously around the world. Television to the child now is what radio is to the adult. With radio the adult has access to news, drama, and entertainment at home without the intermediate step of reading. With television, children have access to news, drama, and entertainment without having to translate words into images. The images are already there.

Television, then, should have special appeal to young children because, like the digital clock, it allows them to do what they could not do with the other media—to extend their senses. The data on television viewing supports this interpretation. Young children watch television the most, and the amount decreases as children get older.[2] This is only, in part, a function of schooling. Adolescents spend less time in school than grade school children, but they still watch less television. Television has somewhat less appeal for the adolescent who has the mental ability to extend his or her senses with radio or print.

Thus television impacts most upon young children, extending their sense experience in ways that were not possible before. It removes many of the intellectual barriers other media put in the way of accessing information. Scenes of violence or of sexual intimacy that a young child could not conjure up from a verbal description are presented directly and graphically upon the television screen. Because television makes so much accessible to children that was not accessible to them before, it hurries children to grow up fast. Young children today can experience events through television that, given other media, they could not experience until a later age.

The situation is comparable to what happened to computer language. As computer language has become simplified (such as BASIC as opposed to FORTRAN) and closer to everyday language, more people can use computers. Television, by simplifying information access, has opened up for children areas of information that were once reserved for adults.

Schools have become so rigidly age-graded that a teacher trained to teach fourth grade must be retrained to teach second or sixth grade. This rigid age-grading reflects a factory model in which each station on an assembly line has its own special function and activity, and a person at one station cannot move to another without further training. Print media tend to reinforce this sort of separation because different curricula can be written for each grade and different job (teacher) descriptions can be written for each station. Print, according to McLuhan, reinforces the individualism of the factory system because reading is, of necessity, an individual, solitary matter.

But television is different. As Louis Kronenberger wrote in 1966:

> *What I think must be said is that television is not just a great force in modern life, but that it virtually is modern life. What, one might ask, doesn't it do? It gives us—be we rich, poor, snowbound, bedridden or slow-witted—the time, the weather, the small news, big news, sport news, now in spoken headlines, now in pictured narrative, now at the very scene of the crime or the coronation itself. It plays, sings, whistles and dances for us, takes us to movies and theaters, concerts and operas, prize fights and ball games, ski jumps and tennis tournaments. It delivers babies, probes adolescents, psychoanalyzes adults. It dramatizes floods, fires, earthquakes, takes you to the top of an alp or the bottom of an ocean or whirling through space; lets you see a tiger killed or a tiger kill. It becomes a hustings, or a house of worship; guesses your age, your weight, your job, your secret, guides you through prisons, orphan asylums, lunatic asylums; lets you see a Winston Churchill buried or a Lee Oswald shot. It teaches you French, rope dancing, bird calls and first aid; provides debates and seminars and symposiums, quizzes and contests and it tells you jokes, gags, wheezes, wisecracks, jokes and jokes.*[3]

Television extends the senses of everyone; it does not discriminate. According to McLuhan, television "retribalizes" us in that "electric circuitry has overthrown the regime of 'time' and 'space' and points upon us instantly and continuously the concerns of all other men. It has reconstituted dialogue on a global scale. Its message is Total Change, ending psychic social economic and political parochialism. The old civic, state and national groupings have become unworkable. Nothing can be further from the spirit of the new technology than 'a place for everything and everything in its place.' "[4]

Although McLuhan probably overstates his case (human inertia being what it is), the homogenization of human experience is certainly a fact. For example, an estimated 700 million people watched the wedding of Prince Charles and Lady Diana. Such a universal experience, and it is but one of many (American television series are popular all over the world, as are certain rock groups), has to have a homogenizing impact. Even in remote small towns, one finds the people reflecting the homogenization of tastes in clothing and food promoted by television.

The homogenization across social, ethnic, and geographical boundaries is also true for age boundaries. Television programs are not rigidly age-graded. Indeed, programs such as "Bewitched" and "The Ghost and Mrs. Muir" have been taken over by children much as stories like *Gulliver's Travels* written for adults have been taken over by children. Even programs such as "Misterogers," "Captain Kangaroo," and "Sesame Street" are watched by a wide age range of children. Television has gone far toward breaking down the rigid age-grading of the schools.

However, television is becoming even more homogeneous than ever before, and this tends to hurry children. The reasons are largely economic, as Geoffrey Cowan points out:

> *To some extent, the sameness and exploitativeness of television—to which so many viewers have a legitimate objection—is a function of the industry's curious economic structure. Unlike other media, such as books and movies—whose revenue comes entirely from consumers—or magazines and newspapers—which derive their income from consumers as well as advertisers—television relies solely on advertising for its revenue. Since the vast majority of companies that advertise on television want to reach an 18 to 49 year old urban audience, there is little incentive to develop programming that appears primarily to people who are older than forty-nine, younger than eighteen or who live in rural areas. If middle-aged or elderly people in a small town in rural America feel that*

television ignores their tastes and offers little that is
nourishing to children, they are right.[5]

In the last few years, commercial television has zeroed in on this eighteen-to-forty-nine-year-old audience almost to the exclusion of all others. For example, even ten years ago there were a number of programs that included young children and, occasionally, their problems in the series. Shows such as "The Brady Bunch," "The Partridge Family," "The Courtship of Eddie's Father," and "Family Affair" included some young children even if they were portrayed as somewhat precocious in wisdom and emotional maturity.

Contrast these shows with those current today in which there are no young children at all. Contemporary series such as "Happy Days," "Laverne and Shirley," "White Shadow," "Eight is Enough," and "Different Strokes" are all primarily concerned with adolescents and adolescent issues. The young man in "Eight is Enough" is precocious, as is the teenager who plays a younger child (Willis) in "Different Strokes." With the exception of a few children's shows and the cartoons, even young children end up watching programs geared to the eighteen-to-forty-nine-year-old age group.

These programs hurry young children because they expose them to the issues and conflicts of grown-ups. However valuable the new realism may be for artistic integrity and presenting the eighteen-to-forty-nine-year-old group with relevant material rather than with fantasy, its impact on children is to hurry them into adult concerns. Consider what happened on television during the seventies:

> *The seventies had been a remarkable period of growth for*
> *the treatment of provocative themes on entertainment tele-*
> *vision. Contemporary material started to be allowed on*
> *variety shows such as* Laugh-In *and* The Smothers
> Brothers Comedy Hour; *then it came full blast in the*
> *serious comedies of Norman Lear, Danny Arnold, Larry*
> *Gelbart, and the Mary Tyler Moore Company; and ulti-*
> *mately it included such fact based dramas as* The Autobi-
> ography of Miss Jane Pittman, Fear on Trial, The Missiles
> of October, Roots, King, *and* Holocaust.[6]

Unfortunately even this brand of realism, artistically done and with socially redeeming qualities, now appears to be passé. "Network executives were less eager to find other producers [like Lear] who could produce socially provocative programs. Network executives were instead trying to replicate the molds that had produced 'Happy Days' and 'Laverne and Shirley' or 'Three's Company' or 'Charlie's Angels.' Social realism was on its way out, 'jiggly comedies,' 'eye candy,' and escapism were coming in."[7]

Whether it was the social realism of the seventies or the "eye candy" of the eighties, young children are seeing more on television than their grandparents ever saw in a lifetime. By homogenizing age groups and appealing to the eighteen-to-forty-nine-year-old audience, television (by omission as much as by commission) treats even young children as grown-up, as part of the large "common" audience. Consequently, even young children seem quite sophisticated about the major issues of our time—drugs, violence, crime, divorce, single parenting, inflation, and so on. What they are able to do with this information is quite another matter. As discussed earlier, television gives children entree into experiences they could never have had without it. Television simplifies experience carried across vast distances and from many different places. Children no longer need to read to learn about places nor do they need to listen and imagine about them—they can experience them directly. But exposure is one thing and understanding is another. Four-year-olds who can tell time from a digital clock still have only a hazy sense of hours, minutes, and seconds. Children still have to go about the laborious process of constructing time units. Making experiences more accessible does not make them more comprehensible.

One consequence of television homogenization for children, therefore, is to create what might be called "pseudosophistication." Children today know much more than they understand. They are able to talk about nuclear fission, tube worms at 20,000 fathoms, and space shuttles; and they seem knowledgeable about sex, violence, and crime. But much of this knowledge is largely verbal. Adults, however, are often taken in by this pseudosophistication and treat children as if they were as knowledgeable as they sound. Ironically, the pseudosophistication, which is the effect of television hurrying children, encourages parents and adults to hurry them even more. But children who sound, behave, and look like adults still feel and think like children.

Children, as we have seen, are not the prime audience of the television programer because they have little money to spend for a very restricted range of goods. Children do not buy cars, furniture, medications, and so on; but they are the consumers of toys, breakfast cereals, and fast foods, and a small portion of television programing is devoted to them. Because the advertising budget is small, the vehicles are inexpensive, namely, cartoons. Saturday mornings have become "Super Saturdays" to millions of children engrossed in what the industry calls "Kid Vid."

Quite apart from the content of the programs, advertising for children also has a hurrying effect:

> 1. *Since children watch over five hours of advertising a week, they see approximately twenty thousand commercials a year.*
>
>   *Advertisers spend over $600 million a year selling to children on television.*
>
>   *The child becomes the advertiser's representative in the home.*
>
> 2. *Are children a proper target for advertising? Research has shown the following:*
>
>   *Many children cannot distinguish TV commercials from TV programs.*
>
>   *Many children believe that all commercials are true.*
>
>   *Many children do not understand the functions of advertising.*
>
>   *Many children don't understand advertising techniques (premiums, disclaimers, camera techniques).*
>
>   *Many older children develop cynicism about commercial messages.*
>
>   *While we may be training skeptical young consumers, are we also suggesting to our children that deception is an approved strategy in the marketplace, that they are entering a world where manipulation and misrepresentation go hand in hand with making a profit?*[8]

By treating children as consumers, television further homogenizes children with adults. When children become the advertisers' "representative in the home," they are encouraged to press their parents to purchase certain products. They are thus hurried into a kind of hucksterism. We as adults are often mislead by children's pseudosophistication about products and may even follow their suggestions or imprecations. Again we get into this vicious circle where television hurries children in a way that in turn causes us as adults to treat them as more grown-up than they are. Television hurries children by treating them as consumers, as if they were adult wage earners with the capacity to see through the deceptions of advertising and to make informed choices.

Television, it has been said, is an "electronic mirror that reflects a vague or ambiguous image. As society is complex and many faceted, broadcasting reflects a variety of images. These are never precisely focused and completely clear. . . . Looking at a blurred or vague image, different individuals see different things . . . television programs mean different things to different people and mean different things to one person at different times, depending upon attitude and mood."[9]

From this standpoint television serves as a way of finding out who and what we are. By identifying with a television character we find out more about ourselves or try and make ourselves more like the character we identify with. How children are portrayed to children thus reflects how society views children and also provides images with whom children identify and seek to emulate. I recall that my middle son always wanted to be like Danny, the redheaded cutup of the Partridge family.

What, then, can we say about children as they are depicted on television? One feature characterizes them all—they are precocious:

> *The children [on TV] are too well behaved and are reason-*
> *able beyond their years. All the children pop in with ex-*
> *ceptional insights. Jody and Buffy of "Family Affair"*
> *repeatedly demonstrate uncanny sensitivity to adult prob-*
> *lems. On many of the shows the children's insights are apt*
> *to be unexpectedly philosophical. The lesson seems to be*
> *"Listen to little children carefully and you will learn great*
> *truths."*[10]

There are additional messages in these depictions of insightful children (such as Alice's son in the "Alice" show, who shows uncanny insight into adult issues). To children they provide models of emotional and intellectual maturity, thus constituting a kind of hurrying to behave in wise, mature ways. And to adults this kind of depiction may add to expectations that children be more wise, more sage, more understanding than we have a right to expect.

BOOKS AND MAGAZINES

Television has had a major impact upon other media that reach children, such as books and magazines: "Television can be credited with the virtual destruction of the very bottom layer of American popular culture—the comic book, the pulp magazine, the radio serial, the hillbilly movie. Newton Minnow's wasteland has been in fact a flood over an abyss which used to be filled by garbage a good deal worse that the featureless rubble of routine television."[11]

Clearly, a comic book like "Bugs Bunny" cannot compete with a television "Bugs Bunny" cartoon; nor can the "Buck Rogers" comic compete with a program such as "Star Trek." The demise of comic books, however trashy, is unfortunate in a way because many children learned to read in order to read the comics. The comics provided a motivation for reading as strong as the child's desire to be up on Saturday morning to watch the cartoons.

The comic book was replaced by *Mad* magazine, which has been in existence for twenty-five years, just about the age of television. "As MAD magazine discovered, the new (television) audience found the scenes and themes of ordinary life as funny as anything in remote Dogpatch. MAD magazine simply transferred the world of ads into the world of the comic book and it did this just when the TV image was beginning to eliminate the comic book by direct rivalry."[12] What is unique about *Mad* magazine is that it provides children not with fantasy but rather with satire. Al Feldstein, editor of *Mad* magazine for its twenty-five-year existence says:

> What we did was to take the absurdities of the adult world
> that youngsters were facing and show kids that the adult
> world is not omnipotent, that their parents were telling the
> kids to be honest, not to lie and yet were cheating on their
> income tax. We told them there was a lot of garbage out in
> the world and you've got to be aware of it. Everything you

read in the papers is not necessarily true. What you see on television is mostly lies. You're going to have to learn to think for yourself.[13]

What is significant about *Mad* magazine is that satire is really only understood when children attain Piaget's stage of formal operations (see page 109). For example, to fully appreciate the *Mad* parody on "Broken Homes and Gardens" which appeared in 1975, the reader had to know about the magazine *Better Homes and Gardens* and the metaphor that "broken homes" stands for "divorce." The child has to appreciate that the parody is making fun of the content of *Better Homes and Gardens* as well as some traditional family values.

Mad magazine, then, is for adolescents, not for children, although the age of readers has been dropping. Originally the magazine was targeted for older adolescents (ages fifteen to seventeen) and college students, but in recent years the mean age of the readership has become about thirteen. And as the readership has grown younger, the material has grown racier. Marie Winn writes: "By the issue of 1980, a parody of *Little Darlings* (a film about two young girls at summer camp racing to see who loses her virginity first) includes an outdoor salesman hawking 'Get your training diaphragms here,' and a little girl spying on a teen age couple and reporting, 'She's starting foreplay now.'"[14]

What has to be understood about *Mad* magazine is not so much its content as its form. Children who have been hurried to grow up fast have many feelings, fears, angers, and anxieties that they are often unable to express. Humor has always been a way of expressing dangerous feelings—almost every joke has some aggressive or sexual content. Thus *Mad* magazine provides young people with some comic relief from the pressures of growing up fast. By making sexuality, drugs, and hucksterism into a joke, young people are able to take distance from some of the stresses of being exposed to too much too soon. *Mad* is a stress relief valve but, unfortunately, only for bright children and adolescents who have the mental ability to appreciate satire.

In the last decade, there has also been a dramatic shift in books for children toward a new realism and a breaking down of many traditional taboos. Books for young children such as those of Ezra Jack Keats, *Whistle for Willie* and *Hi, Cat!*, depict in rich colors and sensitive words episodes in the life of ghetto children. And books by Maurice Sendak created a stir, particularly *In the Night Kitchen* in which the young hero's penis is clearly evident. One cannot really quarrel with sensitive, artistically pleasing books such as these other than to say that the new realism is present even in books for young children. Unfortunately, there are few writers for young children as sensitive and gifted as Keats and Sendak.

There is a lot of tasteless junk for young children being promoted under the guise of the new realism. For example, in one story by Carl Withers entitled *Eenie-Meenie-Minie-Mo* some black bears fall into some white paint. Their mother doesn't know they are hers until they happen to get washed off. The story was, I think, meant to convey the message that "Black Is Beautiful," but the result was just the opposite. Other stories for young children dealing with a variety of delicate themes from divorce to physical and mental disability have appeared in recent years. But there are few writers who can treat these matters with the tact and sensitivity required for young readers.

In the face of the new realism in stories for young children, it is interesting that Bruno Bettelheim has asserted the need of young children for fantasy and fairy tales that are remote from the child's immediate experience. Bettelheim writes:

> *Just because life is often bewildering to him, the child needs even more to be given the chance to understand himself in this complex world with which we must learn to cope. To be able to do so, the child must be helped to make some coherent sense out of the turmoil of his feelings. He needs ideas on how to bring his inner house into order, and on that basis be able to create order in his life. He needs—and this hardly requires emphasis at this moment in our history—a moral education which subtly, and by implication only, conveys to him the advantages of moral behavior, not through abstract ethical concepts but through that which seems tangibly right and therefore meaningful to him.*
>
> *The child finds this kind of meaning through fairy tales. Like many other modern psychological insights, this*

was anticipated long ago by the poets. The German poet
Johann Schiller wrote:
    "Deeper meaning resides in the fairy tales told to me in
my childhood than in the truth that is taught by life."[15]

What Bettelheim has recognized, and what the proponents of
the new realism in young children's literature may have forgotten, is
the emotional, moral side of the young child's life. The new literature for young children pressures them to grow up fast intellectually—to know more about the poor, the disabled, the sick, and the
emotionally troubled. But young children, as Bettelheim has
pointed out, have their own personal agenda, a need to make sense
out of their own lives before they can fully appreciate the predica-
ments of others.

Bettelheim wrote about fairy tales because:

> *I became deeply dissatisfied with much of the literature*
> *intended to develop the child's mind and personality, be-*
> *cause it fails to stimulate and nurture those resources he*
> *needs most in order to cope with difficult problems. The*
> *preprimers and primers from which he is taught to read in*
> *school are designed to teach the necessary skills, irrespec-*
> *tive of meaning. The overwhelming bulk of the rest of*
> *so-called "children's literature" attempts to entertain or to*
> *inform or both. But most of these books are so shallow in*
> *substance that little significance can be gained from them.*
> *The acquisition of skills, including the ability to read, be-*
> *comes devalued when what one has learned to read adds*
> *nothing of importance to one's life.*[16]

Much of the new realism in the literature for young children,
then, hurries them in two ways. The task of self-discovery is more
difficult when children are presented with the problems and difficulties of others before they have had a chance to find meaning in
their own lives. Because many children are never exposed to material like fairly tales, they are deprived of a literature that would
help them make sense and give order to their experience. A basic
maxim of mental health—recognized long before there was anything

like psychoanalysis—is that you have to be able to help yourself before you can help others: "Physician heal thyself."

Young children pushed to be made aware of the whole range of society's ills may not have much chance or opportunity to find themselves. This is the major stress of the literature of young children aimed at making them aware of the problems in the world about them before they have a chance to master the problems of childhood.

The new realism in children's fiction is particularly evident in books for older children and adolescents. A decade or so ago, when I wrote stories for children, it was necessary to read all of the current magazines and books aimed at children to learn what the taboo and overworked topics were. Topics like divorce, venereal disease, physical handicaps, and sexual activity were all prohibited. At that time a salable story had to follow the formula of "an admirable child who struggles to overcome difficult obstacles to attain a socially worthwhile goal."

But children's fiction has come a long way from that simple moral formula. The characters in contemporary fiction for children are not always admirable, at least by traditional moral, social, and gender values. Just as Sendak's *In the Night Kitchen* stirred up controversy in the young children's book field; so did Charlotte Zolotow's *William's Doll,* a tale of a boy who wanted to play with a doll. Likewise, John Donovan's book *I'll Get There: It Better Be Worth the Trip* depicts the two male adolescent heroes briefly kissing during a sleepover. And in Fran Arrik's *Steffie Can't Come Out to Play* the heroine becomes a hooker, takes an overdose of LSD, and is eventually rehabilitated.

So the formula for children's fiction today does not require an admirable character (in the old moral sense) while the obstacles to be overcome are of the new realism variety. According to George Woods, children's book editor of the *New York Times,* he is receiving books that deal with many previously taboo obstacles. "It is not just sex that defines the change. I've got books coming in on children with hairlips, epilepsy, and insanity as well as the usual alcoholic parents, drug addicted children, child beaters, divorce, acne, and death."[17] Apparently authors writing for young people today believe that "anything goes."

Not only have heroes and heroines become less "admirable" in the traditional sense and the obstacles more personal but the goals attained are also less socially meritorious than what was once the case. Previously, in much of children's literature, the goals were often to help or to please others—parents, friends, pets—who were needy or endangered. A boy took risks to save a dog or a girl worked hard to get a desired gift for a sick friend. In children's fiction today, however, the goals are often therapeutic and rehabilitative. Heroes and heroines are healing themselves rather than helping others.

The new realism in children's fiction can be justified in the sense that the old formulas depicted a childhood innocence that never existed in fact. As Charlotte Zolotow, editor of Harper Junior Books, has said: "We can't protect our children anymore from all we would like to spare them. We can't protect them from the war and the violent death they see on television every night. . . . All we can do is to help children to see it all, to form their own judgment and defenses and to be honest in the books we write for them about alcohol, drugs, or immorality."[18]

At the same time, however, it is also important for young people to have imaginative and fantasy outlets. Adolescents, no less than children, need fantasy in order to deal with feelings and emotions that are not always clearly articulated. Nowhere is this better illustrated than in young people's preoccupation with Dungeons and Dragons (D & D), a game in which young people design their own characters and their own conflicts but in a remote historical and geographical setting. In Dungeons and Dragons there are traditional bad guys and good guys, the obstacles are mostly environmental, and the goals are often altruistic in the sense of rescuing someone in distress or danger. It may be that Dungeons and Dragons is one way in which young people can escape from the new realism.

This is not to say that realism in children's fiction is necessarily negative. Certainly, it is one among many pressures to grow up fast. At the same time such fiction does depict the world as it is and may help children prepare for it. What is important is that not *all* fiction for children be realistic. The trouble with the new realism is not its realism so much as its all-pervasive quality, as if to say "realism is good and fantasy is bad." But fantasy, no less than realism, is psychologically healthy. Cinderella, whether dressed up as a "Gothic" heroine or as a contemporary professional woman, is still very popular with women readers.[19] And Robin Hood, dressed up as James Bond, still appeals to male readers. Adults, no less than children, need fantasy as well as reality.

THE MOVIES

Like television and books, the movies have moved toward a new realism in topics, in language, and in characterization. It is hard to believe, in this era of *10*, that there was once a Hayes office, that a couple could not be shown in bed together, and that even words like "hell" and "damn" were forbidden. But the sixties saw the overthrow of most of the moralistic prohibitions and by the seventies we were so used to four-letter words and nudity in films that these hardly needed remarking upon.

As parents became more relaxed about swearing, nudity, sexual activity, and violence on the screen, they also became more relaxed about children watching it. Movies like *Jaws* and *Halloween* not to mention *10* were seen by children of preteen age. With the advent of cable television in both homes and hotels, unsupervised children have access to sexually explicit and violent films. Film ratings, like PG, R, and X, are ambiguous at best and neither parents nor children seem to take them too seriously. Since even X-rated films are available to children at home on late-night cable television, the theater restrictions seem almost silly.

Films, however, impact upon young people in a somewhat different way than television and books. In films there is a rather clear delineation between the actor or the actress and the role portrayed. What may influence children even more than what they see on the screen is the real-life escapades of youthful heroes and heroines. Whether or not Brooke Shields is sexually active offscreen may be more significant to young people than any role she plays on screen.

Thus, in effect, television hurries children much more than film. On television there is much less distance between actor and role, largely because the role is always the same, whereas in films, for the most part, the roles change. With television, children identify with the role, while with film, young people are more likely to identify with the actor. It is when an actress like Tatum O'Neil behaves precociously offscreen that she becomes a model for young women to emulate.

It has to be said that the new realism in the media is somewhat one-sided. To be sure, there is a new freedom to discuss and to depict taboo topics. Children have been liberated along with adults. While this liberalization constituted a kind "freeing of repression" for grown-ups, it may have worked against the formation of such repressions in children. In particular, children today are confronted with all facets of sexuality at an early age. The attitude of parents and the culture in general is that sexuality is okay.

In this respect our culture is becoming a little more European. Films in Europe have always been explicitly sexual than in the United States, as was literature. Europeans took sexuality as a normal part of life, and while it was not flaunted in front of children, it was not regarded as something dirty or to be hidden either. Much as children in Europe were allowed to have a little wine, they were exposed to some facets of sexuality as a preparation for adulthood.

What is so troubling about the presentation of sexuality in the American media today is its "overdone" quality. The "jiggly" series from "Benny Hill" to the "eye candy" of "Charlie's Angels" still presents sexuality as a bit naughty and titillating. We really haven't progressed as far as we think we have or would like. Nudity is present and explicit, sexuality is present, but I am not sure we are more comfortable with it. Indeed, despite our current openness about sexuality, our puritan attitude that it is "dirty" persists.

The real issue that has to be faced in the pressure of media to hurry children into adult awareness of sexuality is whether or not some amount of repression is healthy for the process of growing up. Freud thought so, and not just because he was a Victorian. Freud realized that repression of some instinctual propensities was necessary for social life. If we did not repress some of our sexual and aggressive impulses, we would still be living in a jungle. Even today, sexual liberation is not sexual license. Granted, we are more free and open about our sexuality, but we still are constrained by social rules that regulate sexual behavior. The essence of civilization is rule-regulated behavior.

Realism in the media, then, should not be equated with "anything goes." Part of growing up is learning to control impulses and to behave in socially prescribed ways, which requires time and effort by parents and children alike. When children are exposed to sexual behavior before they know the rules, they are likely to be overwhelmed and totally withdraw or, what is more common, to be pressured by the peer group into behavior for which they are not really ready.

What needs to be understood is that the new realism that pervades the media puts a greater burden on parents, just when they are least able to bear it because of single-parent families, both parents working, and so on. This is true not out of some misguided notion that childhood is a period of innocence that has to be shielded but, rather, that children do need to be socialized and this can only come about through *parental* inculcation of socially prescribed rules of behavior. These rules are built up progressively and eventually become automatic so that the child can behave without awareness of them. The real danger of growing up fast is that children may learn the rules of social license before they learn the rules of mutual respect. In this inverted sequence, sexual exploitation is the inevitable result.

RECORDS

Clearly, the most underestimated influence on young people today is the record business. Perhaps because most adults find the level of sound obnoxious, the harmonics jarring, and the lyrics incomprehensible, we prefer to ignore the impact of rock music on our offspring. As a culture, we are visually oriented, and this is why we are so concerned about the sex and violence presented on television and in films. But music can influence young people as much as any visual media. Philosophers and theologians have long been aware of the power of music: Plato in his *Republic* wanted music censored because he feared its citizens "would be tempted and corrupted by weak and voluptuous airs and led to indulge in demoralizing emotions."

Music promoted for young people is directed not so much to the conscious as to the unconscious or subliminal level of awareness and thus is too easily dismissed. Perhaps more importantly, music directed at young people is aimed not so much at hurrying them into adulthood as at providing escapes from the pressures to grow up fast.

Young people *are* the market for the music industry, unlike television, for whom they are a small part of the market. Producers have broken this market up into discrete segments: the preteen, eight to twelve years old; early teen, thirteen to fourteen; midteen, fifteen to sixteen; late teen, seventeen to nineteen; and postteen, over twenty years old. Interestingly, perhaps because rock music is escapist and defensive, the music producers perpetuate the rigid age-grading of the schools that is so absent in television. Young people are very selective with respect to their preferences, but these preferences are transient like the groups themselves. What seems to be important is that the groups can be used by young people to age-segregate themselves in a way that television does not permit.

That is, the rigid age-grading of our schools gives rise to what I have called an "age dynamism" wherein children look down upon what younger children do and up to what older children do. They want to be like the next older group but not like the next younger group. Hence the constant change in rock groups; as soon as a group is taken up by a lower age group it is given up by the older one being emulated.

The amount of time young people spend listening to the top-forty music stations or to stereo sets has been estimated at six hours daily. Teenagers purchase an average of about four new records weekly and buy 60 percent of all 45 rpm singles. Eighty percent of 45 rpm records are purchased by people twenty-five years old or younger. Unlike television advertising, music merchandising is aimed at the young. More millionaires have attained their wealth from the popular music industry in the last two decades than in any other segment of our economy.

Music for young people suggests escape from stress in three different directions: masturbation, regression to maternal dependency, and the use of drugs. But this is always done in a subliminal, ambiguous way so that teenagers and their parents are not really conscious of the message. There is a great deal of powerful, albeit subliminal, sexual stimulation implicit in both the rhythm and lyrics of rock music. The use of music as a sexual stimulant was suggested in the movie *10*, in which Ravel's "Boléro" was the heroine's choice. But for most teenagers the stimulant is rock music; about a third of a group of male high school students admitted to masturbating while listening to rock music. The real percentage is, in all likelihood, considerably higher. It is no accident that boys frequently lock themselves in their rooms when they turn on their stereos.

Rock music also suggests a regressive seeking after mothering. Most rock vocalists are male and sing songs that are ambiguous as to whom they are addressed. But a mother figure is often suggested subliminally. Presumably young women like these songs because they get vicarious satisfaction out of identifying with the mother cherished by the boy. Rock music has probably set the women's liberation movement back further than any Marabel Morgan (author of *The Total Woman*) ever could. Consider the example of a best-selling song of rock superstar Elvis Presley, entitled "Let Me Be Your Teddy Bear":

> Baby let me be around you every night
> Run your fingers through my hair
> And cuddle me tight.
> Oh let me be your teddy bear.

Why would an adolescent boy want to be treated as his girlfriend's teddy bear? If he was hurried out of childhood with a mother too busy to cuddle him, the record makes sense and speaks to an unfulfilled unconscious need—just what business, the music business in this case, finds appealing.

Paul Anka's "Diana" sold 8½ million copies. Although there was a great search for the real Diana, media critic Wilson Bryon Key says that Anka was really serenading his mother when he sang

> I'm so young and you're so old
> This my darling, I've been told
> I don't care just what they say
> 'Cause forever I will pray
> You and I will be as free
> As the birds up in the trees
> Oh please stay by me, Diana.

According to Key, others from among hundreds of lyrics that utilize maternal identifications include Elvis Presley's "(You're So Square) Baby I Don't Care"; Joe South and the Believers' "Walk a Mile in My Shoes"; Bobby Vee's "Rubber Ball" and "Sharing You"; and Frankie Avalon's "Welcome Home."[20] Apparently Al Jolson was but one of a long line of singers who sang out for motherly love and affection. The contemporary versions of "Mammy" are just more disguised.

Even more discouraging and frightening is the way in which rock music has been promoting drug use. While researchers and congressional committees have been debating the effect that television has upon children (coming up with no clear conclusion), another question is of much more significance to the lives of our young people—what was the Beatles' contribution to Western society? The answer, according to Key, is simple but shocking: "The Beatles popularized and culturally legitimated hallucinatory drug usage among teenagers around the world."[21]

In this connection Key's analysis of the Beatles' 1968 recording "Hey Jude" is instructive:

> *Two meanings for "Jude" appeared as likely symbology in the song. "Jude" could have referred to Judas who betrayed Christ under the guise of friendship. Heroin, of course, at first seems to be a friend before it betrays the user into addiction. The second possibility involved the apostle Jude who warned against those who call themselves Christians while living hypocritically in a morally loose society.*
>
> *The haunting voice of McCartney sang "let her into your heart." Her, meaning the drug and "heart" the pump that circulates drug laden blood through the body—so "you can make it even better."*
>
> *During the lonely opening verse, the drug injection occurred. In the second verse, musicians joined to make the sound [life] more full and complete. The lyrics tell us, "Don't be afraid" the moment you "let her under your skin," you begin to make it better.*
>
> *The third verse said ... "anytime you feel the pain. Hey Jude refrain."*
>
> *"Refrain" means in one sense, leave it alone. But the inverse symbology means repeat the chorus or repeat the injection at the end of each good period when the pain returns. The verse explained that only a fool pretends there is nothing wrong with empty feelings and avoids being helped by the heroin.*
>
> *The narrator, or drug pusher, repeats his plea in the fourth verse asking "don't let me down." All you need do is "go and get her" and "let her into your heart."*
>
> *The fifth verse advised, "let it out and let it in." Or let out inhibited emotions and feelings, let the drug or syringe into your body. "You're waiting for someone to perform [synonym for trip] with. Don't you know it's just you. You*

are all that is necessary. The movement you need is on your shoulder." Suggesting either the arm used for injection or the monkey on your back or shoulder.

The final verse counseled "don't take it bad," a bad trip should be avoided, "make it better" by releasing inhibitions and fears. Toward the end of the song, a scream is heard for "Mamma," a cry for help, a plea for rescue from the drug addiction.

As the song progressed, a screaming maniacal chant is heard in the background—providing a contrapuntal theme to the lyric. The chorus chanted "you gotta break it"—an apparent reference to the habit—"you know you can make it." "Don't go back" or, in other words, stay clean.[22]

The ambiguity of the lyrics is intentional. Studies of adolescents' understanding of the lyrics of the songs they buy and listen to suggest that less than 25 percent really comprehend what a song like "Hey Jude" or "Tommy" is all about—at least at the conscious level. Rather, they say they like the sound and the way "it makes me feel." And yet the message, like most advertising messages, is getting across at the subliminal level.

Another example of a song that could be interpreted as pushing drugs is Paul Simon's hit "Bridge Over Troubled Waters." Although only about 15 percent of a group of adolescents cited the "I" of the narrator as a drug pusher, a strong case can be made for that interpretation. As Key writes: "If the 'I' or the singer is a drug pusher, what he is describing in the song is a drug trip, his customer—or audience—is the young audience bewildered by the fast paced automated, depersonalized, lonely, complex, and powerful society." The following is Key's analysis of the song:

In the first verse the music begins with a lone piano chording (like a spiritual as suggested by Simon). The spiritual piano is sustained throughout the arrangement. . . . In the second verse the listener is still "down and out" but now "on the street." The street of life where the troubled water swirls, the place where society rushes frantically to nowhere, the street is loud, impersonal and cold. The pusher promises "when evening falls so hard, I will comfort you."

> *Evening is symbolic of death and darkness, perhaps the colorlessness of American society.*
>
> *The pusher declares his willingness to "take your part" become the audience, suffer for them while they escape through drugs. "When darkness comes and pain is all around" the pusher will provide "a bridge over troubled water."*[23]

In the third verse the term "Silvergirl" is introduced which is an adolescent slang term for hypodermic needle, and the lines "your time has come to shine" followed by "All your dreams are on the way" clearly suggest a drug trip. And the "If you need a friend, I am sailing just behind" indicates that the pusher is always there with another fix when it is needed. The last sentence of the third verse carries what Key calls the drug pusher's pitch line "I will ease your mind."[24]

Rock music, then, would seem to provide young people with escapes from the pressures of growing up fast, from the feeling of meaninglessness and emotional loneliness which such pressures produce. Free-floating anxiety is reduced through masturbation; longings to be loved, to be taken care of, to be cuddled and held are expressed in haunting lyrics; and the pain of facing reality head on is reduced by the promise of drugs. It is perhaps a bitter irony that we adults turn away from and ignore the music our children listen to, because in this music and the ambiguous lyrics, young people seek escape from an unhappy world adults seem hell-bent to rub their noses in.

Part II

Hurried Children:
Stressed Children

Chapter 5

Growing Up Slowly

*T*he concept of hurrying implies that there is a slower, more normal and healthier pace to growth and development than many American children currently enjoy. This chapter will describe some of the achievements, and some of the limitations, of the major stages of development—infancy, early childhood, childhood, and adolescence. In addition, the chapter will spell out some of the effects hurrying has upon the "normal" course of intellectual, emotional, and social development.

Swiss psychologist Jean Piaget has described four major stages in the development of children's thinking. Piaget argued that at each stage children do not copy what they encounter but actively construct reality out of their experiences with the environment. The realities constructed by children are, in a sense, a series of progressive approximations to adult reality and so do not coincide point for point with the adult vision of the world. Moreover, prior to adolescence, children lack the mental abilities to think, reason, judge, and make decisions in the way that adults do. These capacities are developed in stages as well. In short, both the content and form of children's thinking changes with age.[1]

In recent years, evidence has been accumulating in support of the stages described by Piaget. The tests he devised to reveal the stages have now been used in more than half the countries in the world with amazingly comparable results. Children all over the world go through these stages, at least up to adolescence. In addition, Herman Epstein of Brandeis University in Boston has recently compiled data to show that brain growth after birth occurs in "spurts" at just the ages at which Piaget postulated major transformations in children's thinking.[2] There is, therefore, considerable evidence to support the stages of development as described by Piaget.

The Piagetian stages, however, will only be the framework for the description provided below; included is discussion about children's social-emotional development as well. Once we see and understand the strengths and the limitations of each stage of development, the meaning of hurrying and its dangers will become more obvious.

THE SENSORI-MOTOR PERIOD

From birth until about two years of age infants are concerned with constructing a world of permanent objects, attaching themselves to significant others, and establishing what now retired Harvard professor Erik Erikson called a sense of "trust."[3] These three attainments constitute the major intellectual, social, and emotional developments of the infancy period.

With respect to permanent objects, young infants have no idea that objects continue to exist when they cannot see, hear, feel, taste, or smell them. What we as adults experience as objects, cups, saucers, dogs, cats, and so on, are in part concepts that we have constructed. We know that a particular cup does not exhaust the class of cups and that cups exist all over the world regardless of whether we are able to see or touch them. But our knowledge about cups, like our knowledge about dogs, cars, houses, and boats is not innate; we did not come into the world with this knowledge but had to acquire it.

How does this acquisition come about? Traditional psychology said that children looked at the cup and abstracted its common properties or features. The problem with this position is that it presupposes the knowledge it seeks to explain. If children could distinguish a cup well enough to abstract its common features, they would already have the concept they were supposed to be obtaining. The abstraction theory of knowledge acquisition is circular.

Piaget argues that objects such as cups are not perceived as distinct entities by children but, rather, must be constructed by them. Only as children look at, touch, drop, push, and grab a cup do they

begin to conceive of it. Their conceptions are based upon their actions with the cup, their active exploration of it, not passive looking
and abstracting. This is why it is so important for infants to explore
their world by looking, touching, feeling, tasting, grabbing, and so
on. Through these activities infants construct concepts of objects
such that they understand by the end of their second year that cups
and other objects continue to exist when they are not looking at
them.

This development is easy to demonstrate with both animate and
inanimate objects. When Piaget's daughter Jacqueline was eight
months old, Piaget held a cigarette case in front of her and then proceeded to let it fall to the floor. Jacqueline did not follow the trajec-
tory of the case but continued to look at his hand. She had not yet
formed a concept of a cigarette case that would enable her to follow
it when it fell. By the time she was nineteen months old, however,
Jacqueline gave evidence that her conceptualization of objects was
now well advanced. Piaget placed a coin in his hand and then placed
his hand under a coverlet where he let the coin drop before removing his hand. Jacqueline first looked in his hand and then immediately lifted the coverlet to find the coin.[4]

A similar construction occurs with respect to people. Young
infants do not believe that people, any more than objects, continue
to exist when they are not present to the senses. In one study, for example, infants of three months and ten months of age were compared for their reactions to a few days of hospitalization for minor
surgery. When the three-month-old infants returned home, they
showed few adjustment problems and quickly fell back into the routines they had followed before they left. In contrast, the ten-month-
old infants showed signs of acute anxiety, clung to their mothers,
and did not settle down for several weeks. It is not surprising that
fear of strangers and reluctance to be with baby sitters also appear
at this time.

According to English psychologist John Bowlby, infancy is also
a time when children form their primary attachments to caretakers.[5] These attachments—the mother is usually the prime attachment figure—depend in part upon the infants' construction of the
mother as an object. But they also reflect much more: they reflect a
basic need for attachment, to relate in an emotional way to another
person. The child's attachment to the mother is a powerful motivation of much of the child's learning. Attachment makes it possible

for the infant to enjoy love and caring (which mean nothing if they come from someone to whom the infant is not attached) but also to fear separation and loss.

In addition to specific attachments, infants must also establish a sense of trust. Children have the potential for trust and distrust, and which predominates depends upon their early experience. The infant who finds the world a dependable place, whose needs are met on time and in a consistent fashion, acquires a sense of trust that goes beyond his or her immediate caretakers. It becomes a sense of trust, a sense that the caretakers are good and reliable—a sense that is eventually extended to people in general. Conversely, an infant whose caretaking has been sporadic, who has been neglected, may develop a sense of mistrust of the world as a fearful and dangerous place where no one can be depended upon.

Infancy, therefore, is a very important time because it is the period when children not only develop their basic concepts about the world, but also when they form their most critical attachments and social orientations. These achievements, like those that come later, take time and effort and cannot be rushed. Becoming an adult person does not happen all at once, and the quality of the person that develops will depend, in part, upon the quality of time and effort expended during infancy. This does not mean that infants should not be placed in day-care centers or left with sitters. It does mean (as we shall examine in detail when we consider contracts) that infant needs should not become subordinate to parental needs.

THE PREOPERATIONAL PERIOD

The years from about two to six are momentous ones in the child's development toward full personhood. From the intellectual standpoint it is a period when children acquire the symbolic or representational function and can now represent, in conventional or original ways, the objects and relations they have constructed during the years of infancy. The acquisition of language permits children to express their intellectual discoveries and their wants and feelings directly. In addition, as they become socialized and recognize their relative powerlessness, discover dangers, and encounter unpleasant people and experiences, they begin to express fears and anxieties in dreams and in symbolic play. The fascination that super heroes (such as Superman) have for some children is a case in point. Super heroes demonstrate the weaknesses and limitations of the average adult. They help children overcome the belief that parents are all powerful and all knowing.

In addition to the symbolic function, young children also acquire elementary reasoning powers in relation to symbols. They begin to form concepts of classes of objects and of general relations that go beyond the specific acquisitions of the infancy period. But children at this stage also make characteristic mistakes having to do with the one and the many. When young children see a dog and say "dog," it is not clear whether they mean "look at that black cocker spaniel," the specific dog, or "look at the dog," at a particular example of the class of dogs. When young children call a strange man "Daddy," they give evidence of a confusion between words that stand for one object, "Daddy," and those that stand for many, "man."

Children at this stage also become attached to symbols in much the same way that they become attached to objects and people. Young children are even more attached to symbols than are older children and adults. For example, young children get very upset when they are called by the wrong name. Thus you may hear children in a nursery school or day-care program call each other by full names. Full names—Harry Brown, Helen Pickett—insure that two children with the same first names will be clearly identified.

The attachment to and investment in symbols helps explain why it is difficult for young children to separate from people and things they consider their own. Young children resent a new baby in the family because, in part, they conceived of the symbolic "mommy" as belonging to them alone. Indeed, the mother is seen almost as a part of the self, so giving her up is like giving up part of the self. The same is true for toys: children have difficulty sharing not because they are selfish in the adult sense but because sharing something that is part of the symbolic "me" is like sharing part of the self.

The symbolic function also gives rise to a kind of word magic. Children believe that if they are called a bad name such as "Stinky," they receive the property along with the name. Children also believe that events that happen together cause one another. A child will become attached to a blanket or teddy bear that brought comfort once, and which the child now believes "causes" or necessarily brings about comfort. It is this kind of magical thinking that makes young children believe that they are responsible for parental separation or divorce. The child believes that some act that he or she committed coincident with the time of the separation caused the separation. Such thinking can be the cause of long-standing guilt and anxiety.

Early childhood is also a period—in the Eriksonian scheme —during which children either enhance their sense of autonomy or bring their feelings of doubt and shame to the fore.[6] If children are permitted to make decisions that are appropriate for them to make—when they need to be toileted, for example—they develop a healthy sense of being able to take responsibility and make decisions. If they are requested to toilet themselves too soon, before the motor control has been developed, they will have accidents and experience shame and doubt about their ability to control their behavior, make choices, and take charge of their actions. Whether a child acquires a healthy sense of autonomy or is burdened with excessive feelings of shame and doubt depends upon the skill with which parents match their demands to the child's competencies.

Around the age of four or five, children must deal with their sense of initiative versus their sense of guilt. Children of this age have acquired considerable motor control, language ability, and intellectual competence. They are curious about their world and eager to explore it, and their curiosity is expressed in endless "Why" questions, such as "Why does the sun shine?" or "What happens when you get to the end of the earth?" Children at this age also like to take things apart (like old clocks, toasters, or radios) to see how they work.

The sense of initiative, curiosity, and exploration is encouraged when parents take time to answer children's questions, when they provide opportunities to explore and discover, and when they do not get unduly upset by the frequent messes that result from their child's attempts to initiate their own understanding of the world. On the other hand, if children's questions are answered cursorily or not at all, if parents are too busy to provide exploration opportunities and become angry at the scattered parts of old telephones, clocks, or radios after an exploratory foray, the child may develop a sense of guilt about his or her sense of curiosity and desire to explore.

Children need time to explore in a responsive environment in order to acquire a healthy sense of initiative. When children are hurried from one day care center or caretaker to another, there is no time to explore, and when the environment is not responsive—par-

ents are too busy or too tired to respond to their children's questions—the children's sense of guilt about themselves and their
exploratory actions far exceeds the healthy sense of initiative, the
sense that it is okay to be curious and wondering. The sense of guilt
established in early childhood provides a lifelong orientation that
can inhibit the young person's initiative in his or her dealings with
the social as well as the physical world.

THE CONCRETE OPERATIONAL PERIOD

At around the age of six or seven, children attain a new set of mental
abilities that Piaget calls "concrete operations." Like the symbolic
function attained in early childhood, concrete operations enable
children to do many things they could not do before. In particular,
they are now able to operate upon symbols in the way that they
learned to act upon and manipulate objects in infancy. For example,
once children attain concrete operations, they are able to classify in
a hierarchical way. They now grasp that boys and girls are included
in the class of children; that cats, dogs, and mice are animals; that
pianos, violins, and tubas are all musical instruments. Children can
now manipulate symbols for things in the way that they once manipulated the things themselves.

There is an important difference between the manipulation of
things and the manipulation of symbols. The manipulation of symbols is mental and goes on in children's heads; it does not involve
their hands. To illustrate, if a four-year-old is shown a finger maze (a
large wooden maze that permits the child to explore alternate paths
manually), the child proceeds to explore it with his or her finger,
moving it along the different paths until the one that leads to the exit
is discovered. When the maze is given to a six-year-old, in contrast,
the child does not explore it manually at all but explores it visually,
finding the correct path and only then putting his or her finger to
the maze. In exploring the maze visually, the child is mentally ma-
nipulating the maze with the aid of symbolic rather than manual activities. Symbolic manipulation vastly extends the range and variety
of explorations the child can perform.

The capacity to manipulate symbols mentally makes possible a
whole new level of achievement that was not possible for preschool
children. Unfortunately, however, our language does not give us
markers for these new achievements and so they are often missed.

Consider the child's conception of number, for example. Young children may be able to discriminate correctly two or three things and use the terms *two* and *three*. But for them, *two* and *three* are simply names, such as the numbers on a football player's jersey. It is only at the age of six or seven that children attain a true sense of number. At that age they recognize, for example, that a set of twelve objects, such as the forks, knives, and spoons used to set the table for four people, remains twelve whether they are arranged on the table or bunched together in the dishwasher.

Advanced reading, like advanced number understanding, is quite different from beginning reading, although again our language provides no markers of the difference. We talk about children reading or not reading as if the issue were one of black and white, as if there were no shades of grey in reading. But there are many shades of grey in the attainment of advanced reading skills. The young child who has memorized all the words in a book has learned to sight-read, but like learning the numbers *two* and *three,* sight-reading is a much simpler intellectual activity than decoding new words and using syntactic structure to infer meaning. This level of reading does not usually occur until after the age of six or seven.

These levels of competence are often ignored when children are hurried. When parents do not distinguish between beginning and advanced levels of number and reading skill, they can mistake one for the other. "If," I hear some parents say, "she knows her numbers (can count to ten), why isn't she doing arithmetic?" Or, "If he can read this sentence (such as "I have a turtle" in a book with one sentence per page), why can't he start on *Robinson Crusoe?*" Learning to efficiently manipulate symbols mentally takes time and can't be rushed if the child is to become truly competent.

Concrete operations make possible new interpersonal as well as intellectual attainments. Children at this stage, for example, have the capacity to learn and operate according to rules, the basis for all lasting social exchange. Learning to operate according to rules requires a kind of syllogistic reasoning that is made possible by concrete operations. For example, in order to learn to use *please* or *thank you* correctly on particular occasions, the child must reason as follows:

"Whenever someone gives you something you must say *thank you.*"

"This person has just given me something."

"Therefore, I must say *thank you.*"

The child is not aware of going through this reasoning process; it is part of what Piaget calls the "intellective unconscious." Much of our thinking is unconscious and we are usually only aware of the results. This is one reason we have so much trouble understanding the difficulty children encounter in learning such things as rules. Once we have mastered rules and syllogistic thinking, we are no longer aware of using these processes in our interpersonal exchanges. It seems to us, for example, that children should learn to say *please* and *thank you* after being told to do so a few times. To adults, saying *please* and *thank you* seems to be a simple matter of memory, not reasoning. We say to children "Remember to say *please*" or "Remember to say *thank you*" as if learning rules were a matter of memory alone.

The ability to learn rules makes formal education possible, because most of what children learn as they acquire the basic skills of reading and arithmetic are rules. They learn phonic rules (long $\bar{a}$ with a silent *e*) and spelling rules (*i* before *e* except after *c*) and arithmetic rules (when you add horizontally, $49 + 55 = 104$, you move from left to right; when you add vertically, you move from right to left). Mastering the basics means acquiring an enormous number of rules and learning to apply them appropriately. Hurrying children academically, therefore, ignores the enormity of the task that children face in acquiring basic math and reading skills. We need to have a better appreciation of how awesome an intellectual task learning the basics really is for children and give them the time they need to accomplish it well.

Learning rules also makes it possible for children to play games that presuppose complex rules and to create their own games and rules. One of the dangers of organized team sports for this age group is that they no longer have the opportunity to create their own games and rules and thus to acquire a healthy sense of the relativity of rules. I recall seeing a group of boys racing along the street when one yelled, "Last one to the corner is a nerd." One unfortunate youngster was tripping over his sneaker laces and had to stop to tie them. He shouted to the first boy, "Not included!" To which came the swift reply, "No say-backs." Learning to create rules—even simple rules for otherwise uncomplicated street games—and to abide by those you have created is an important part of rule learning and of mature social behavior.

Children who have attained concrete operations are also able to enter the culture of childhood which is, in effect, a body of rules that has been handed down by oral tradition over hundreds of years. Sayings such as "Step on a crack, break your mother's back" or "Rain, rain go away, come again another day" or "Finders, keepers; losers, weepers" make up part of the language and lore of childhood. Learning the sayings, the superstitions, the jokes and riddles of childhood are the initial stage of social interaction among peers who share common ways of looking at and dealing with the world. Hurried children are often deprived of this rich cultural heritage and the opportunity to interact with peers on a level that is unique to childhood and removed from adult concerns.

I am not advocating a romantic view of childhood that suggests that this period is free of conflict and anxiety. There are conflicts and anxieties that are appropriate to this age period—concerns about peer acceptance and about academic and athletic competence—that have to be faced and dealt with. What is crucial during this period is that young people learn to deal with peers on an equal footing as persons with reciprocal needs and interests. This is different from dealing with an adult where the relationship is unilateral—that is, adults have more authority than children.

One consequence of single-parent families and of families with working mothers is that parents and children sometimes interact on a mutual footing. Calling parents by first names, as is common today, reflects this development. Perhaps that is why, in part anyway, we have organized sports at the elementary school level. The family once provided the superordinate-subordinate system of relationships while peers provided that of mutuality and equality, but the reverse seems to be happening today. Parents deal with their children as equals, whereas peers, at least in sports, have to recognize that some age mates (for example, the captain of the team or the quarterback) have more authority than others. Through such inversions peers can come to have more authority than parents.

From a social attachment point of view, childhood marks the first partial separation from parents and the beginning of new attachments to other adults and peers. This comes about, at least in part, because of concrete operations. Young children tend to think of their parents as all-powerful and all-knowing, godlike creatures. When children attain concrete operations, however, they have the mental capacity not only to reason but to check symbols against experience. They begin to distinguish between, for example, fantasy and reality and give up their belief in Santa Claus and the Easter Bunny. (It is perfectly okay for young children to entertain these ideas; giving them up provides children with a useful marker of intellectual development—"I don't believe in that anymore.") But they can now also discover that parents make mistakes and say things that the child knows are not true.

This discovery that adults are not perfect and the resulting deflation of their godlike state is nicely described by art critic Edmund Gosse in his childhood memoirs:

> *The theory that my father was omniscient or infallible was now dead and buried. He probably knew very little; in this case he had not known a fact of such importance that if you did not know that, it could hardly matter what you knew.*[7]

Once parents are removed from the pantheon of gods, children are able to elevate other adults to that status. During the elementary school period, children often idealize sports figures, movie stars, and young musical performers. They also begin to talk about being "in love" with a peer, about having "boyfriends" or "girlfriends" although in fact there is not much boy-girl interaction during this period.

Another consequence of the dethroning of parents is a phenomenon that I have called "cognitive conceit." When children catch their parents in an error (as Gosse did), they assume that if the parent did not know that simple fact, then the parent doesn't know anything. Furthermore, the children also believe that if they know something the parent does not know, then they must know everything. They must be smarter than their parents and, by extension, adults in general. It is not surprising that children of this age tell jokes and favor stories that put adults in a derogatory or stupid role. Dagwood Bumstead, the bumbling, forgetful, impulsive, work-avoiding character of the comic strips, provides a nice portrait of the child's view of the adult. Interestingly, Dagwood's children are portrayed as more adult and mature than he is.

Cognitive conceit is thus one outgrowth of the school-age child's beginning emancipation from parents. Although cognitive conceit is a normal phenomenon of childhood and usually does little harm other than providing children with amusement (they love to laugh at adult errors of any kind), it can have more serious consequences. Hurrying children into decision making that is more appropriate for adults plays into the child's cognitive conceit. When adults ask children to help them make critical decisions in their lives—about moving, remarriage, changing jobs—the children's sense of cognitive conceit, of being smarter and wiser than adults, is reinforced. This can give children an inflated notion of their own wisdom and power and can bring them grief later.

The beginning detachment from parents also makes possible, in late childhood, the establishment of what psychiatrist Harry Stack Sullivan called chumships—close friendships between children of the same sex wherein the pair share their most intimate feelings and thoughts. Sullivan believed that it is essential for children to establish a sense of intimacy that would be the basis for all future relationships with persons of both the same and the opposite sex. The hurrying of children can sometimes have the consequence of robbing them of the opportunity and time for chumships.[8]

Finally, from an Eriksonian point of view, the period of childhood is the time when children establish either a firm sense of industry—that they can do a job and do it well—or an abiding sense of inferiority, a sense that whatever they undertake will end badly. Because of the changed attachment conditions and because children now spend long hours at school, parents are no longer the primary arbiters of the child's sense of industry or inferiority. This has both positive and negative potentials.

If, for example, children have parents who undermine their sense of industry—by, say, complaining about everything they do around the house, jumping upon their every mistake, and ignoring what they do well—their sense of inferiority may come to outweigh their sense of industry. However, should these children encounter a teacher who senses their capabilities, gives them opportunities to work, and reinforces their achievements, the children may acquire a healthy sense of industry in spite of, rather than because of, the treatment they received from their parents.

Unfortunately the reverse is also possible. Parents who make every effort to instill a healthy sense of industry in their children may find their efforts undermined by a school that is too bent on hurrying children into academics to acknowledge individual differences. Children who are confronted with demands to do math or to read before they have the requisite mental abilities may experience a series of demoralizing failures and begin to conceive of themselves as worthless.

Such children not only acquire a sense of inferiority that overwhelms their sense of industry but also may acquire what Martin Seligman of the University of Pennsylvania calls "learned helplessness."[9] When humans or other animals are confronted with a series of situations over which they have no control and wherein any efforts they make toward control are ineffectual, they become quiescent and no longer make efforts to master their environment. As we shall see later, children who experience repeated school failure are likely to acquire the orientation of learned helplessness as well as an abiding sense of inferiority. While parents can prevail against the school's impact in this regard, they may not be successful.

Childhood, then, is a period when children have attained concrete operations, can learn rules, and are ready for formal schooling. It is also a period when children are beginning to detach themselves from parents and during which time other adults and peers become more important. Particularly in late childhood, close "chumships" pave the way for future intimate interpersonal relationships. Finally, childhood is also a period when the balance between industry and inferiority is determined by the child's experiences at both home and school.

FORMAL OPERATIONAL PERIOD

As children become adolescents, around the age of eleven or twelve, the physical changes in height, body configuration, and facial proportions are so dramatic that they often mask the equally dramatic changes that are going on in children's thinking. Indeed, Piaget's discovery of the new mental abilities occurring in early adolescence constitutes one of his truly momentous discoveries.[10] While it has long been recognized that by age six or seven children attained the "age of reason," it was not recognized that there are quite distinct levels of reasoning. In effect the reasoning engaged in by children is of a different order than adolescent reasoning. It constitutes nothing less than a Copernican revolution in how children see the world.

In addition to the intellectual changes, emotional and social changes occur as well. Attachments to parents and to others become more complex and undergo fundamental transformations. Relative dependence is transformed into relative independence in the emotional, intellectual, and social domains. And adolescence is also the period that Erikson describes as critical for the establishment of a sense of personal identity that must overshadow a sense of role diffusion. All of these achievements of the adolescent period can be affected by hurrying.

The intellectual attainments of adolescents are considerable. Just as the child is able, thanks to concrete operations, to manipulate objects by means of symbols, the adolescent learns to manipulate symbols with higher-order symbols. For example, when we talk about a noun or a preposition, we are talking about symbols. The language of grammar is a second-order symbol system in which the terms represent classes of symbols rather than classes of things. It does not, therefore, make a lot of sense to teach children grammar, since they cannot really deal with it in any intelligent way until they have attained the new mental abilities that Piaget terms "formal operations" and that permit young people to deal with symbols for symbols.

However, children can certainly use grammar correctly before they can think about it in an abstract way. Young children, for example, use correct word order, tenses, plurals, and so on before they can talk about what it is they are doing. Language itself is a symbolic process. To talk about language rather than things requires a new level of language comprehension and, in effect, a new language—the language of the grammarians. But this language can only be understood by those with formal operational thought. The ability to do something does not imply the ability to talk intelligently about what is being done.

Piaget gave an interesting experimental demonstration of this phenomenon when he asked children of various age levels to first walk on all fours and then to describe what it was they were doing. Although young children were much more adept at walking on all fours than were older children and adults, they were much less adept at verbally describing it. Only the adolescents and adults could say, "First I move my right hand, then my left hand, then my right knee, then my left knee." Right and left are symbolic relations, and to talk about them successfully requires formal operations.[11]

Algebra is still another illustration. In an algebraic equation —$(a + b)^2 = a^2 + 2ab + b^2$—the letters represent numbers. Algebra, like grammar, is a second-order symbol system that represents a first-order symbol system. Second-order symbol systems permit the manipulation of first-order systems. Metaphor and simile are of second level because they are symbols for symbols. A proverb such as "Shallow brooks are noisy" is a metaphor because its symbols, shallow brooks, do not represent the actual things, shallow brooks, but rather other symbols—shallow individuals. Most young people do not really appreciate simile and metaphor until they are adolescent. Thus children read *Alice in Wonderland* and *Gulliver's Travels* as straight stories, and adolescents read them as allegory.

Much of our thinking is also symbolic, so that although children think, it is not until adolescence and the appearance of formal operations that young people think about thinking. It is at this time that words which symbolize thought products and activities begin to appear in young people's vocabulary. Teenagers, in contrast to children, begin to talk about what they "believe" and "value" and about "faith" and "motives." Thinking about their own and other people's thinking is a unique achievement of adolescent mental operations.

Formal operations also enable adolescents to conceptualize or reconceptualize past and future in new ways. Parents, for example, are often amazed and distressed to hear themselves bitterly castigated for some slight the young person incurred as a child—"you bought him a new bike and you didn't buy me one"—which was not remarked upon at the time. But in adolescence such memories are elaborated and embellished with the aid of formal operational thinking. Now young people can conceptualize and attribute motives to their parents' behavior that they only intuited before. Many painful memories of childhood are resurrected and reinterpreted in adolescence. Hence young people begin, in adolescence, to pay their parents back for all the real or imagined slights parents committed during childhood that were suppressed or repressed—but not forgotten.

This is an important point in the context of this book. Children who are hurried as children may not understand or resent the hurrying until they become adolescent. Then they may begin to be angry and resentful at parents for reasons the parents find hard to fathom. Many of the problems and behaviors of adolescents have their roots in childhood experiences that are only resented at the time but reacted to later. This "sleeper" effect of hurrying children occurs because adolescents acquire new mental operations that enable them to recast their early experience in terms of parental motivations and intentions.

Thanks to formal operations, young adolescents also construct what I call an "imaginary audience." Now that teenagers can think about their own and other people's thinking, they nonetheless make a characteristic error. They confuse what they are thinking about with what other people are thinking about. Because of the dramatic changes taking place in their bodies, in their feelings and emotions, young people concentrate upon themselves. Consequently, they assume that others are as concerned with their appearance, their feelings, and their thoughts as they are. This is the imaginary audience, the belief that others are as concerned with us as we are.

The imaginary audience, which is most prominent in early adolescence, has powerful motivational force. The characteristic self-consciousness of young adolescents derives, in large measure, from the imaginary audience. You become self-conscious when you assume that everybody is looking at you and thinking about you. For example, young adolescent males who, as boys, had to be forced to take baths and wash themselves begin showering and washing their hair every day of their own volition. The hours spent by young people in the bathroom and the affinity of this age group for mirrors of whatever kind and in whatever place also speak to the power of the audience.

The presence of an imaginary audience helps to explain why some young adolescents react more strongly to separation and divorce than children or older adolescents. The young adolescent may believe that everyone not only knows about the divorce but also about some of the more unpleasant reasons for it. The young person feels embarrassed that everyone knows about the family's personal life and bitterly resents his or her parents for what is experienced as a humiliating public exposure.

A common, indeed universal, imaginary-audience fantasy is that which involves imagining the audience's reaction to our own demise. When we are feeling low, sad, sorry for ourselves, we take pleasure in such audience constructions. It is a way of "stroking" ourselves when there is no one else to do it for us. Recall the passage from *Tom Sawyer* in which Tom sneaks back to his home, after having run away with Joe and Huck, to discover that he and his friends are thought to have been drowned:

> *But this memory was too much for the old lady and she broke entirely down, Tom was snuffling, now himself—and more in pity of himself than anybody else. He could hear Mary crying and putting in a good word for him from time to time. He began to have a nobler opinion of himself than ever before. Still he was sufficiently touched by his aunt's grief to long to rush out from under the bed and overwhelm her with joy—and the theatrical gorgeousness of the thing appealed strongly to his nature too—but he resisted and lay still.*[12]

While we all engage in such fantasies at times, we are usually aware of what we are doing. But my impression, in encounters with adolescents who subsequently committed suicide, is that the imaginary-audience fantasy can play a part in such acts. Indeed, children who are hurried by being exposed to a real audience at an early age—perhaps because of the negative or positive achievements of their parents that puts them into the tabloids and in the public eye—may construct more powerful imaginary-audience fantasies than children who have been less exposed. Such young people are more at risk for suicide. If a young person feels at the mercy of an all-powerful audience and feels that the audience is disapproving, he or she may commit suicide in an effort to punish the audience and make it suffer for the mistreatment that it meted out. The following case history (from my personal file) illustrates this sequence of events:

> *A young man of sixteen, Harry Y., committed suicide by stealing drugs from a doctor's office, taking them, and then concealing himself in the ticket booth at the high school stadium so that he could not be found. He had been born in Germany to an army sergeant who married a German girl. When Harry was five his father, in a jealous frenzy, murdered his wife and killed himself. Harry went to live with*

an aunt in Colorado. The aunt had a poor marriage herself and Harry was taken in largely because of the government checks that came for his support. From an early age, Harry was left to fend pretty much for himself. He was pressured to grow up fast out of neglect.

Despite his history and difficult living situation, Harry was doing reasonably well in school, was on the track team, and was seeing a girl from a well-to-do and happy family. A track meet was coming up and Harry asked his aunt for money to buy some new track shoes. She refused. Harry asked her several more times, always with the same result. The last time, he lost control and swore at her abusively. Unbeknownst to Harry, his girl friend's mother was in the next room. When she appeared and Harry realized that she had heard him, he was appalled, fled the house, and broke into the doctor's office for the drugs. He was not found until several days later.

Adolescent suicide is but one possible consequence of the heightened power given to an imaginary audience when children are hurried to grow up fast.

Other hurried youngsters, those who from an early age have engaged in competitive sports or in the performing arts, and who have been exposed to real audiences as children, nonetheless still construct an imaginary audience when they become adolescents. Indeed, the audience they construct may even be more powerful than that constructed by young people with a less-exposed personal history. As a consequence, they may become supersensitive and extremely overconcerned with their appearance and performance to the point of refusing to engage in their professional activity. The opposite result can also occur, and the young person may become overly vain and conceited, relegating himself or herself to the level of superstar. Many child "prodigies" who have been pushed by their parents face a "mid-life crisis" in early adolescence when they have to deal with the imaginary as well as the real audience.

Closely tied to the imaginary audience is another construction which I have called the "personal fable." If everyone is watching you and is concerned with your behavior, then you must be something special, something unique upon this earth. The fable leads us to believe that other people will grow old and die but not us, other people may get sick but not us, and so on. Indeed, when personal tragedy strikes us, as it does everyone, one of our first reactions is "this could not be happening to me, these things happen to other people, they are not supposed to happen to me."

The concept of a personal fable helps to explain a great deal of adolescent risk-taking and also why hurried children are more likely to take risks than nonhurried children. The personal fable is, in effect, a belief in one's own invulnerability. "It will happen to somebody else, not me." This is a very adaptive concept because there is so much to fear in this world that if we did not operate on the assumption that we were relatively immune from danger, we would never step out of the house, ride in a car or airplane, or eat any packaged food. We would be immobilized. But there is also a danger in taking one's fable too seriously, and when this happens young people take unnecessary risks.

The examples of this phenomenon are well known: the young woman who fails to use contraceptives and who does not demand this precaution of her partner partly in the belief that it destroys the spontaneity but also under the conviction that "other girls get pregnant, not me." In the same way, the young man who experiments with stronger drugs after trying marijuana is convinced that "other kids get hooked, not me." And other young people cheat or steal at school because, to some extent, they believe that "other people will get caught, not me."

Why do some young people invoke the fable and take risks while others do not? While the answer is complex, I believe that hurried children are more seduced by the fable than nonhurried children. Basically (as discussed in more detail later), hurried children are stressed children. Under stress, people become more self-centered, more egocentric than when not highly stressed. Now the fable is an egocentric concept—it amplifies the individual's sense of uniqueness and invulnerability. A stressed young person thus has a heightened fable and is therefore more likely than a less-stressed person to act upon the fable, ignoring the factual knowledge of the risks involved. Although this personal fable is counter-intuitive, young people under stress are likely to be more impulsive risk-takers rather than more cautious ones.

In addition to these changes and events triggered by formal operations, other events are occurring in adolescence as well. The parents, who were once the primary attachment figures, now find themselves eclipsed as young people become attracted to members of the opposite sex. When this happens young people often feel guilty. It seems to them that when they "fall in love" they are, in a way, being disloyal to their parents. They behave as if love existed in a fixed quantity and that if you give some love to someone new, you have taken it from an old love.

Young people are not always aware of this dynamic, but they are aware of the guilt. They may get angry at their parents and find fault in all kinds of ways in order to assuage this guilt. Adolescents suddenly discover that their parents don't know how to walk or talk, how to dress or eat. Now that adolescents have developed formal operations they can construct ideal parents and compare them with their own, whom they usually find sadly wanting. When this happens they do not need to feel guilty about taking love away from parents who are not that great anyway.

In this regard, then, children are no different from adults. When an adult breaks off a relationship, he or she often demeans the other person in order to ease the guilt associated with the withdrawal of love. Children, of course, eventually discover that there is enough love to cover *both* parents *and* a friend or marriage partner. But this understanding comes in late adolescence and early adulthood. In early and middle adolescence, young people still have a need to find fault with and to be critical of their parents.

Among hurried children, who may harbor a lot of anger at their parents, the criticism and fault-finding may often be more cutting and exaggerated than it is among young people who do not harbor long-standing grudges against their parents. Freud called such anger that was out of proportion to its immediate object "overdetermined." The anger that hurried children express toward their parents is actually directed not at the parents' clothes or eating habits but at a long series of real and sometimes imagined abuses. The anger of hurried children sometimes goes beyond verbal criticism and, in extreme cases, can result in physical attack.

The final dimension of adolescence that needs to be covered is what Erik Erikson calls the "crisis of personal identity versus role diffusion." Formal operations make possible, among other things, the construction of theories. A theory is a second-order symbol system, and in this sense algebra could be said to be a theory of mathematics, and grammar a theory of language. Both are abstractions and operations upon the primary-symbol systems. What we call "personality," "personal identity," or "self" is a theory in this sense. A personality is a higher-order abstraction that encompasses lower-order abstractions seen as feelings, attitudes, traits, habits, and so on, some of which may be contradictory. Thus a personality is a theory about how the disparate facets of a given person mesh together and make sense.

It is not until adolescence that young people construct a sense of personal identity, of having a unique personality. Nor do young people attribute personal identity or personality to other people until adolescence. The construction of a sense of personal identity requires, in addition to formal operations, some consistent experiences of self. Young people who have a consistent sense of their sex role, their success as students, their work habits, and their relations to adults and to their peer group find that constructing a personal identity is a challenge and a rewarding task. The ingredients are all there, they just need to be put together once the requisite mental operations are attained.

On the other hand, if young people are unclear as to their sex role, unsure about their academic competence, and ambivalent in their relations to parents and peers, the construction of a sense of personal identity can be severely inhibited. In effect it is hard to construct an overriding theory of personal identity when the data are inconsistent and discrepant. When this happens young people experience a sense of "role diffusion," a lack of clear definition and cohesion that may lead to adopting a negative identity (such as a criminal or prostitute) in which the definition is clear or unambiguous. Other young people may choose a loss of identity in the subjugation to a cult or religious organization such as the "Moonies." The attraction of such groups is that they provide a preformed identity that the young person can assume without struggle and regardless of his or her personal history.

It is my sense that hurried children have problems with attaining a secure sense of personal identity. In the case of young people who have been immersed in athletics or the performing arts, identity formation comes too early. Such young people tend to define themselves quite narrowly, in terms of their accomplishment and not in terms of the many social and intellectual facets that we usually associate with personality. Likewise, children who are hurried into mature decision making and responsibility may have a distorted sense of their powers and capacities in this regard. Their sense of personal identity may appear more mature and secure than in fact may be the case. These ramifications of hurrying will be explored in more detail later.

For the moment it remains to reiterate the major argument of this chapter, namely, that growth into personhood in our contemporary society takes time and cannot be hurried. As we know it, growth occurs in a series of stages that are related to age. Each stage brings dramatic changes in intellectual capacity, in emotional attachments, and in social relations. The elaboration of these new capacities in all of their complexity and intricacy is a slow and deliberate process. When children are pressured to grow up fast, important achievements are skipped or bypassed, which can give rise to serious problems later.

Chapter 6

Learning to be Social

*J*ust as children have traditionally been seen as "plants" that "unfold from within" or as "raw material" that has to be "shaped from without," families have also been looked upon in metaphoric terms. One view of the family is that of a "haven in a heartless world," a sort of refuge from the trials and tribulations of the competitive world.[1] The notion of "a man's home is his castle" captures this "refuge" image of the family that has also been promoted by some American sociologists, namely, Talcott Parsons.[2]

A second, contrary image of the family is that it is not so much a refuge as a "prison" that promotes the worst rather than the best in its inmates. People imprisoned in family life become emotionally ill or socially disruptive. In socialist and authoritarian countries, the family is often seen as the enemy of the state, and communal child-rearing is a way of lessening its debilitating effects. Even in democratic societies such as our own, the family has often been attacked by social scientists, such as psychiatrist R. D. Laing, as a breeding ground of neurosis and psychosis.[3] At one time or another, American families have been attacked for "momism," for "permissiveness," or for putting children into "double binds" (for example, the mother who says, "Come give me a kiss," but whose body language says that she finds the child offensive).

To some extent, of course, every family is both a haven and a prison. Both parents and children retreat to the security of the family at times of stress or catastrophe. When a parent or a child is seriously ill, for example, the family is the center of this person's support system. Nonetheless, each family member may at some time chafe at family responsibilities that interfere with personal plans or activities. With respect to children, however, the family is always more than just a haven or a prison, it is a school of human relations in which children learn how to live within a society. Discussed in this chapter is the family's human relations training function, how it socializes children, and how stress encourages parents to speed up the educational pace.

How does the family socialize children? At least four different answers to this question have been given by psychologists and sociologists. The "social learning" theorists argue that children learn largely by "modeling" adult behavior. If parents are well socialized, law abiding, and respectful of authority, their children will be too. On the other hand, if parents take liberties with the law and are rebellious, their children will do the same. Social-learning theorists, such as Albert Bandura at Stanford University, have been particularly concerned with television violence because of its potential effect upon children who can be expected to "model" the aggression.[4]

A second approach to socialization is that of "behavior modification" which derives from the work of B. F. Skinner and his students. According to this point of view, socialization comes about as a matter of rewards and punishments. Parents who reward their children for learning and obeying rules and who withhold rewards when rules are broken will have children who can adapt to the larger social order. In contrast, parents who do not reward rule-regulated behavior, or who reward rule breaking, will have children who defy the social norms.[5]

Still another way in which socialization by parents has been explained is by "social cognition," a position stimulated by the work of Jean Piaget. According to this view, rules vary in their logical complexity and some rules are easier to understand than others.[6] Parents who gear their teaching to the child's level of understanding will have a much better chance of success than those who disregard rule difficulty. An alternative approach, suggested by some investigators, is that mental development be accelerated by training so that children can learn difficult rules earlier.

The last position is that of Freud's psychoanalysis.[7] In psychoanalytic terms, a child becomes socialized by means of identification and internalization. The boy, for example, identifies with (sees himself as like) the father and progressively internalizes the father's values, beliefs, and prejudices. Likewise, the girl identifies with the mother and progressively internalizes the mother's values, beliefs, and prejudices. Freud did not discuss the processes of identification and internalization at great length, but he meant something more than simply modeling—it was an elaborate process of incorporation that came about as part of emotional identification.

Each of these theories of social learning contains a certain amount of truth. Human beings are complex, and in all probability we learn things in more than one way. Children sometimes do learn by modeling; one has only to hear a nursery-school child at play say with perfect adult inflection, "If you do that again, I'll break your arm!" to be aware of a child modeling adult verbalization. Likewise, rewards and punishments do work sometimes but always in more complex ways than we would like to suppose. And symbolic rewards, like a pat on the head or a loving word or look, are much more potent than objects in reinforcing behavior.

It is also true that children's learning of rules is limited by their level of cognitive understanding, as suggested in the last chapter. On the other hand, while some efforts to accelerate children's intellectual understanding have had limited success, the majority of studies give evidence that efforts at accelerating intellectual development have little if any lasting value. Finally, we know that children also learn by identification and externalization, because as adolescents and adults they may reveal values, beliefs, and prejudices that they never revealed as children but which can easily be traced to parental influences when they were young.

The "contract" model of socialization to some extent incorporates all of the positions presented above. This model argues that socialization always presupposes implicit, usually unverbalized, and unconscious reciprocal expectations on the part of children and their parents. The nature of the expectations varies with the age of the children and the sensitivity of the parents; hence, the "social cognitive" dimension of child-rearing is especially taken into account by the model.

Fulfillment of the contracts is often symbolized by specific rewards and punishments employed by the parents. When rewards and punishments work, it is not because of the immediate pleasure or pain they entail but, rather, because of what they symbolize about underlying contracts. For example, if children believe that what they have done (such as cleaned up their room) deserves a reward and the reward is not forthcoming, they will be upset. But they will be upset by the fact that their good behavior went unrecognized rather than by the lack of a specific reward such as money or a special privilege. Thus rewards and punishments are important to children not because of their intrinsic (immediate) value but because of their symbolic significance.

Modeling behavior is also part of this contract theory insofar as parents often contract with their children in the same way in which they have experienced contracts. All parents have at one time or another caught themselves saying something to a child in a tone and with words that echo tones and words that they experienced as children. Modeling thus adds to the quality and content of contractual interactions between parents and their offspring.

Finally, the identification and internalization suggested by Freudians are probably the mechanisms by which children come to incorporate contracts and make them their own. In contemporary writing, however, identification can mean "attachment," a kind of emotional bonding between parent and child. Internalization can today be seen as a kind of "reflective abstracting" activity whereby the child abstracts the nature of the contracts from a series of parental acts. What the child acquires by this abstraction is not a set of specific behaviors but a general rule or sets of rules that govern classes of behaviors.

As discussed in the last chapter, children usually do not learn rules, such as those of games like checkers and dominoes, until they attain concrete operations. However, this does not mean that young children cannot learn rules but only that they cannot learn them by verbal instruction. Even young children can learn rules from adults by abstracting from adult behavior. It is likely that children learn language rules and many other rules that govern their behavior in everyday social situations through reflective abstraction; the children can acquire these rules because they are demonstrated rather than explained. Young children can also learn rules implicit in parental behavior even though they cannot learn comparable rules that are presented verbally.

PARENT-CHILD CONTRACTS

From a developmental position, reality is always relative in the sense that it is a joint product of the individual's intellectual activity and the materials provided by the environment. In the realm of physical reality, for example, the child's conception of the conservation of number—the notion that the number of elements remains the same despite their physical arrangement—requires both an experience with objects and reasoning activity. This is true because enumeration is more than a perceptual judgment. It is just about impossible, for example, to determine by sight how many jelly beans there are in a glass candy jar that is full to the brim.

The same premise holds true for social realities, although they are more complex because stimulus cues such as facial expression and voice intonation are much more subtle. Children must construct with their mental ability and from their social perceptions a social reality that will enable them to survive both within and outside of the family.

There is, however, a sense in which social reality is different from physical reality. At least initially, the child's discovery of physical reality is immediate—it is derived directly from contact with physical objects and events. The child's discovery of social reality, however, is always mediated by parents and caretakers. Mediation means simply that parents and caretakers act upon the child to mediate his or her construction of social reality. A child who smiles and is smiled upon acquires a different social reality from a child who receives a different reaction. The physical world, by and large, does not react differentially to the child, but the social world always does. (Children also condition parental reactions and realities, so that socialization is never one-sided.) Hence, from his or her first moments of life, the infant's social experiences are mediated by the particular caretakers in the environment.

The fact that social reality is mediated by particular caretakers does not mean that its construction is totally capricious. Constancies in the construction of social reality exist in the implicit expectancies that both parents and children carry with them; and these constancies result in "collective realities" that have some commonalities from family to family. Collective realities, constructed anew with each child, are what I call "parent-child contracts."

Contracting is complex and goes on at several psychic levels at the same time. For example, children who are supported for a particular achievement may come to believe that all support is contingent upon that achievement or a particular level of success. I knew a girl who drew horses very well, for which she was much complimented, but then she was afraid to draw anything else. Sometimes, too, children may believe that parents expect more from them than they really do. One boy I saw as a client was terribly relieved to discover that his parents did not really expect him to get straight A's on his report card.

On the other hand, if parents fail to support children in a given achievement, the children may feel that they were not successful enough, that they did not do enough—in short, that they were at fault. An adolescent boy of my acquaintance joined a cult because he felt that he could "never do enough" to please his parents. Contracts, then, particularly interpersonal ones, can be misread and misunderstood by both the parent and the child. Violations of contracts, real or imagined, are stressful to children and adults. As discussed later, the pressure to grow up fast is often seen by children as a violation of a fundamental contract—the right to grow at one's own pace and time—and hence is experienced as stressful.

The freedom-responsibility contract is fundamental in all parenting. Parents, recognizing the initial helplessness of infants, expect that as children grow they will progressively be able to take responsibility for their own behavior. But the parents must sensitively monitor the child's level of intellectual, social, and emotional development in order to provide the appropriate freedoms and opportunities for the exercise of responsibility. Consequently, as children mature, the freedom-responsibility contract is rewritten again and again. In effect, parents and children construct and reconstruct their collective realities. When this is not done, significant interpersonal damage can occur. But when there is a reasonably close match between parental expectations and child performance and between child expectations and parental performance, there is relatively little stress in family interactions. Contractual violations, hence stress, occur when parents do not reward responsibility with freedom or when children demand freedom without demonstrating responsibility.

The following examples illustrate how the freedom-responsibility contract operates. When children are infants, parents do not expect much in the way of responsibility, and they grant few freedoms. Infants are closely monitored. But parents do have some expectations that emerge as soon as infants want to do things for themselves. When, for example, an infant wants to feed himself or herself, the parent is likely to permit it as long as at least some of the food gets in the baby's mouth.

In early childhood, children become mobile and want to take liberties for which they may not be ready. A young child may, for example, want to lift a glass or plate that the parent feels sure will be dropped. It is critical for the parent to be able to assess adequately the child's competencies, which often involves a little trial and error and a few broken plates. (Substituting plastic for glass or ceramic dishes can make this trial and error less traumatic for parents.) As long as children understand that they will have more chances later, withholding freedoms after some exploratory failures can help children assess the limits of their own competencies.

During infancy, and to some extent during early childhood, the parent-child contract is generally communicated absolutely. The parent decides whether or not a particular freedom should be allowed, and the child has little recourse other than an emotional reaction to the parental dictate. In later childhood, however, because of the language facility and reasoning powers of school-age children, contractual arrangements become more relative. Children will often not accept a unilateral judgment by the parent and will argue their cases for particular freedoms, such as staying up late or eating junk food, with considerable vehemence.

It is at this juncture that parenting styles become evident. One can define the typical categories of parenting—democratic, authoritarian, or laissez-faire—with respect to their treatment of contracts. Democratic parents listen to the child's argument, give their own reasons, and make a judgment that takes the child's position into account. Authoritarian parents will not entertain the young person's arguments for a particular freedom and continue to make unilateral judgments. Laissez-faire parents, however, are persuaded by the child's argument and may grant freedom without demanding responsibility in return.

In adolescence, parent-child contracts reach new levels of complexity. Contracts become abstract or general and merge with moral and ethical principles as well as with the laws of the larger society. The use of the family car, for example, is controlled in part by the parents' understanding of the young person's responsibility but also by his or her age and the possession or lack of a driver's license. Smoking marijuana and drinking are also regulated, to some extent, by both parents and society. What seems to happen in adolescence is that the freedom-responsibility contract becomes one between the child and society, as well as one between parents and offspring. Thus the freedom-responsibility contract prepares the young person to become a responsible member of the larger society.

To illustrate, my middle son, Bob, who is fifteen, wanted to take a bicycle trip to Montreal with some of his friends. We sat down and went over the plans the group had made. I discovered that they had carefully planned their route and where they were to stay each night. They also had a plan for communicating regularly with parents. They had sufficient provisions, first-aid kits, and spare tubes for the trip. Finally, the young men who were planning the trip were high school seniors and in my judgment seemed like careful and responsible young men. It was at that point that I gave my son permission (and money!) to make the trip. The boys made the journey without incident and had a very enjoyable time.

The freedom-responsibility contract in adolescence becomes complex in still another way: parental power over adolescents' freedom is much more limited than it was over the freedom of children. Children can generally be controlled by parental words, but this is not the case for adolescents. Parents can tell their adolescents not to smoke, drink, or have sex, but this may often have little or no effect upon adolescent behavior, particularly if parental contracting during childhood was arbitrary or inconsistent. Young people who move into adolescence without a good sense of the freedom-responsibility contract are more likely to take freedoms that are unsecured (by appropriate demonstrations of responsibility) than children with a strong sense that freedom is earned by responsible behavior. In my experience, many young people arrested for drunken or reckless driving have not been well parented in the freedom-responsibility contract.

The freedom-responsibility contract is one that is often violated when children are encouraged to grow up fast, for example, by being given freedoms for which they may not be fully prepared, like staying home alone. What happens then is the children usually acquire the responsible behaviors required to adapt to the freedoms they were provided. But acquiring these responsible behaviors may be stressful and may be attained at the expense of other activities necessary to well-rounded growth, such as play and fantasy activities.

A second type of reality that is constructed between parents and children involves achievement and support. Parents generally have certain expectations about children's achievements that they support cognitively, affectively, and materially. Again, these contracts have to be rewritten as children mature and as the kinds of achievements of which they are capable begin to broaden. Parents, too, have to extend the types of support they provide for their offspring.

A few examples may help to make the evolution of this contract more concrete. During infancy, parents expect largely sensorimotor achievements of their offspring, and their supports are largely affective. When infants begin to hold their heads up, stand up in the crib, or say a recognizable word, parents respond with hugs and cries and other affective signs of approval. In such ways, children quickly learn that achievement, or attempts at mastery, are rewarded by parents.

During the preschool years, sensorimotor achievements are coupled with symbolic achievements, and affective supports from parents are coupled with symbolic rewards. Young children not only begin to master their bodies but also their clothing, eating, and toileting. They also begin to master language, and parents who could not wait for the child to speak now cannot wait for him or her to be still. In addition to the affective supports of infancy, parents frequently add the symbolic supports of the preschool period—such phrases as "very good," "nicely done," and "look at that."

Childhood achievements become more differentiated as children enter school. Achievements are then evident in three domains: the academic, the interpersonal, and the extracurricular. Unlike the achievements of infancy and the preschool years, these achievements have a social dimension and involve interaction with teachers, peers, and other adults. At this stage, children are not as totally responsible for their achievements as in the years of infancy and early childhood. It is important that parents appreciate this interaction and recognize that children's success or failure in these domains is not entirely their doing.

Parents, in turn, expand the range and nature of the supports that they provide in this period. There is, for example, an increase in the amount of material support as children are provided with clothes and supplies for school and money and equipment for extracurricular activities. Among middle-class parents, at least before the energy crisis, parents showed support by driving their children to friends' houses, to lessons, and so on. Parents also begin to show support by their presence at certain activities, particularly when the child is performing in a school or extracurricular event. As children's achievements become more social, they expect parental support to be more public.

The importance of parental presence as a support for children's achievements should not be underestimated. It is a clear sign that the parents care when they take the time to come see their children perform, particularly when the children know that the parents are not there for their own pleasure or enjoyment. This awareness of parental presence is even true among preschool children although in a somewhat muted form. I remember visiting my middle son's nursery school class, at the request of his teacher, so that I could observe a "problem child" in the class.

It so happened that as I was sitting and observing, a group of boys, including my son, sat in a circle nearby. The conversation went like this:

> Child A: *"My daddy is a doctor and he makes a lot of money and we have a swimming pool."*
> Child B: *"My daddy is a lawyer and he flies to Washington and talks to the President."*
> Child C: *"My daddy owns a company and we have our own airplane."*
> *My son (with aplomb, of course): "My daddy is here!"*
> *with a proud look in my direction.*

Children regard the public presence of their parents as a visible symbol of caring and connectedness that is far more significant than any material support could ever be. The most expensive gift will never replace the parent's presence at a child's birthday party.

In adolescence, academic, interpersonal, and extracurricular achievements are expected, and parents become more particular in their demands within these domains. They may expect adolescents to do well in certain courses, they may not be pleased with any of the adolescent's friendships, and some extracurricular activities may be frowned upon. In adolescence, for the first time, parents and their children may not agree on what sorts of achievements are most valuable and important.

In addition, particularly in middle-class families, young people often become enmeshed in "achievement overload." So much emphasis has been placed on achievement that young people overload their schedules: a child may be taking ballet and piano lessons, playing in the softball league, doing volunteer work in the hospital, and still may be carrying a full course load in school. Many of these young people have to keep date books because their time is so tightly scheduled. Even committed and caring parents find it hard to support all of these activities, and parent-child conflicts often ensue over "cutting back."

Achievement overload often occurs because the child has misread the parent's support of achievement. When young people assume that parents are concerned only with how well they do, rather than with who they are, the need to achieve becomes addictive. True meaningful support should communicate to children that achievements are supported because they are *good for the children*. Then the children recognize that what they are doing is for their own good and not just for the parents. When children feel that achievement is for the parent, not for the self, they either eventually give up or go into achievement overload to assure continuation of parental support.

Adolescents continue to need the same sort of support they required when they were children. They still consider it support when a parent attends a play or concert in which they are participating. And adolescents still need affective support; despite their size and physical maturity, they still need a hug, a pat, a cuddle or two. We never grow too old or too big for this kind of support. Such affective support communicates that the parent is supporting the child as a person that the parent likes and loves, not just the attainments the young person has been able to achieve.

129

A third collective reality constructed by parents and children involves implicit expectations regarding loyalty and commitment. In general, parents expect a certain amount of loyalty from their children in return for the time, energy, effort, and expense the parents expend in the children's upbringing. As in the other contracts, however, the realities have to be reconstructed as children and parents mature. Indeed, parents must come to expect new loyalties consistent with the child's expanding sense of self and world.

During infancy, as discussed previously, children progressively construct a world of permanent objects that are conceived as existing when they are no longer present to their senses. At the same time, infants also begin to construct a notion of self as existing in time and space. Parents intuitively come to expect that during infancy their offspring will be loyal to them as objects, showing attachment, fear of separation, and so on. Indeed, whereas much has been written about fear of separation as a sign of attachment, it is also an expression of loyalty for parents. The infant who refuses to respond to strangers gives the mother or father, or both, an important and gratifying sign of his or her loyalty to them.

A recent personal observation helps to amplify this point: A young faculty wife brought her infant son to our offices at the university. Everyone, the secretaries and other faculty members, made much of the baby, commenting upon his curly hair, his blue eyes, and so on. One of the secretaries asked if she could hold the baby, and the mother said yes. But as the other women held out her arms to take him, the baby began to cry and cling to his mother. The mother was apologetic but at the same time held the baby a little closer, and there was a special, pleased look in her eyes—the satisfaction of knowing that her baby *knew* he was her baby. To the mother, I am sure, this was an expression of the child's loyalty to her.

As infants move into early childhood, they begin to construct a world of signs (conventional representations such as language) and symbols (personal representations such as dream images) to signify and extend their control over the object world. Consequently, the child also constructs a notion of the symbolic self associated with the words "I," "me," and "mine" with his or her name and with the family name. At this stage, parents begin to expect, in addition to loyalty to themselves as persons, a loyalty to the symbols that they represent. Parents, for their part, show commitment in the amount of time and concern they put into child-rearing. Children monitor very closely how much time parents spend with them and for them.

The birth of a sibling causes a crisis in the loyalty-commitment contract because, with pregnancy and the birth of a new sibling, the parents' commitment clearly becomes divided. Indeed, one way of looking at sibling rivalry and birth-order effects on personality is to consider the ramifications of siblings on the loyalty-commitment contract.

As children attain school age they construct a world of rules, and a "lawful" concept of self as a rule maker, follower, and breaker. The parental conception of loyalty must expand to include these new constructions, and children's loyalty is now measured in terms of the extent to which they abide by the rules. When school-aged children lie and take things, parents become angry, in part, because they see these actions as disloyalty to them. Just as parents expect children to be loyal to the symbols they represent, they expect their children to be loyal to the rules (values, beliefs) that they espouse.

When young people reach adolescence, they become capable of higher-level modes of thought and new conceptions of the world and of the self. The new world that is constructed is ideological in the sense that young people become enamored with and capable of dealing with abstract ideas. But they also construct a concept of the reflective self that can think about itself, as well as about the thoughts of others. Not surprisingly, the kinds of loyalties parents expect change too. Parents want young people to be loyal to parental beliefs and values as well as to them as persons, to family symbols, and to moral rules. For example, parents may consider the dating of someone from an ethnic or religious group of whom the family disapproves as a sign of disloyalty.

The adolescent's newfound ability to construct ideals and contrary-to-fact conditions sometimes produces a crisis in the loyalty-commitment contract in the following way: The adolescent constructs an image of ideal parents who are perfect in every way. He or she then compares this ideal parent with the real parent and finds the real parent sadly wanting in appearance, manner of dress, personal habits, and so on. Such criticism is seen by parents as a lack of loyalty.

Young people who have been pressured to grow up fast often feel a lack of commitment by their parents and are more likely than those who have not been hurried to be critical of their parents. Hurried children may feel that parents are more committed to their own lives, careers, and friendships than they are to the child, who is hurried. When they reach adolescence, young people feel no need to be loyal to the parents as people nor to the values and beliefs they espouse. When young people feel that parents have violated a contract, they feel no obligation to fulfill their part of the mutual obligation.

The peer group, a youth cult, adherence to a rigid discipline like vegetarianism, or joining a different church than the parents fills the vacuum left by giving up parental values and beliefs. The power these alternatives have over the young person is in direct proportion to the extent to which he or she feels a lack of commitment on the part of parents. One of the overall negative effects of hurrying children is the damage it does to the loyalty-commitment contract. Although the damage may be done in childhood, the consequences often only appear in adolescence.

This is a brief description of the kinds of realities that I believe parents and their offspring construct in the process of living and growing with one another. It is just a framework for looking at how we go about teaching our children to be social. How does a child who has been on one side of the freedom-responsibility, achievement-support, and loyalty-commitment contracts come to be on the other side when he or she becomes a parent? Although a simple modeling of parental behaviors can provide part of the answer, it really does not tell the whole story, because contracts involve a whole series of implicit expectancies that may never be modeled directly and that are communicated in complex and subtle ways. Modeling is too simple to account for the intricate transformations that take place.

It seems to me that one has to look at the interpersonal patterns that evolve in childhood and adolescence for the answer. Relationships to parents tend to be unilateral in the sense that parents expect responsible behavior in return for which they grant freedoms. Children are not in the position to demand that parents act responsibly, and they cannot give freedoms. Thus it is unlikely that children learn the parental side of contracts by modeling their own parents' behaviors.

I believe that children learn the other side of contracts with other children and with siblings. Here the relationship is one of mutuality; it is not unilateral. In playing and working with other children, young people can begin to expect certain behaviors in return for certain favors. In childhood, the rewards for obeying contracts are most often personal acceptance. For example, a child that shows he or she is willing to abide by the rules of the game is permitted to play. It is with peers that children learn the reciprocal nature of contracts and how to be on the giving as well as on the receiving end.

This is perhaps most clear in adolescence when strong and abiding friendships are formed. In such friendships, one can discern contracts that have mutuality as their basis. In true friendships, for example, each friend supports the other's achievements. On a football or hockey team, everyone embraces the player who gets the winning point, but they would embrace any player who did it. This is a clear case of reciprocal achievement support.

In close friendships, loyalty and commitment are also apparent. Commitment is shown by working at the relationship, trying to be together; and loyalty is shown by defending it against those who would break it up. In the same way, good friends may advise one another about their actions, about the responsibilities inherent in certain freedoms. Thus friendships during childhood and adolescence are critical to the attainment of adult competencies, in particular, those dealing with the intimacy of marriage and parenting.

CONTRACTUAL VIOLATIONS AND HURRYING

Thus far I have described what usually occurs in two-parent families in which one parent stays home for part or all of the time. In contemporary families, however, in which both parents work or when there is only a single parent, the orderly progression of contractual learning is altered. In such families, children learn the reciprocal roles not through friendships in adolescence but largely by the demand of circumstances and parental pressure. Requiring children to play the reciprocal role in contracting is the most powerful mechanism by which parents can hurry children.

Some contractual violations that encourage hurrying occur in two-parent families when both parents work. In such families, children may be given certain freedoms—to make their own breakfast, choose their own clothes—before they have demonstrated responsible behavior in these areas, such as choosing nutritious foods and putting on clothes appropriate to the temperature and time of year. It was clear to me that some children are not ready for these freedoms when I was asked to see a young girl of eight who brought empty ice cream cones in her lunch pail and wore a halter and shorts in the middle of a harsh northeastern winter.

Similarly, working parents sometimes expect achievements beyond what young children may be capable of; demands for achievements in the social domain may be among the most inappropriate. As suggested earlier, some children may be expected to adapt to three or four different social settings during the same day—to a nursery school, a day-care center, and a baby sitter. Such a child is being supported for achievements that require a level of social maturity and adaptability that few young children possess.

Finally, working parents may sometimes violate the loyalty-commitment contract by expecting children to be loyal in the adult sense of the term. I once witnessed the following event in a day-care center: A working mother had come to pick up her three-year-old daughter, Penny, at about 3:30 P.M. It had been a difficult day at the day-care center with one emotional crisis after the other. Through it all, Penny went about her business despite the turmoil swirling around her. When Penny's mother arrived, Penny was sitting near a day-care worker. As soon as she saw her mother, she grabbed the day-care worker by the neck and clung on for dear life; she also began to sob, violently.

The mother was, of course, both appalled and embarrassed. She was appalled because, despite the commitment she felt she was showing by working so her daughter could have a better life, the daughter showed no loyalty. She was also embarrassed because her daughter seemed to prefer another adult to herself and because it seemed that she had provoked an emotional outburst in her child just by her very presence. In talking to the mother, I tried to explain that Penny could not really appreciate her working for the welfare of the family—the child only understood that her mother left her for long periods of time. As for Penny's emotional outburst, it was occasioned by the mother but not in the way the mother thought. Only when Penny saw her mother could she let go of her control and express the fear, anger, and anxiety she had been controlling all day. It was because she felt secure in her mother's presence—the true test of loyalty—that she allowed herself an emotional outburst.

Clearly, families in which both parents work are here to stay, at least for the near future. Nothing that has been said here should be taken as advocating that one parent stay home to take care of the children. However, the demands of two parents working should not blind us to children's built-in limitations of responsibility, achievement, and loyalty. So long as we arrange our lives and our children's lives so that they are not given inappropriate freedoms, not expected to achieve beyond their limits, and demands are not made for unconditional loyalty, parents can both work and still not rush their children into growing up fast.

Another contractual problem sometimes occurs in two-parent homes, most often with respect to girls but sometimes with respect to boys. The situation usually goes something like this: While the girl is growing up the parents may be quite democratic and give her freedoms to the extent that she shows responsibility. This may even involve wearing makeup and designer clothes at an early age, so the girl has a sense of growing up fast and of having her parents' support and encouragement for this process.

However, when the girl becomes adolescent, starts to menstruate, and shows breast development, some parents panic. These parents switch parenting styles and become authoritarian although they were once democratic. Now the girl is told that she cannot date, for example, until she is fifteen, regardless of how responsibly she has behaved. The girl feels that this is a contractual violation because up until this time freedom was granted on the basis of demonstrated responsibility. Now suddenly, and usually without discussion, a relative contract has become an absolute one.

Actually, the problem is more general than has been portrayed in the above example, and it provides one of the major stresses experienced by hurried children. Many young people who have been accustomed to dressing and talking like adults are often frustrated as adolescents because the maturity imposed upon them as children is thwarted. While adolescents today are apparently more sexually active than in past generations, they are still restricted by law from smoking, drinking, driving, and working, at least until they are sixteen. Parents and other social institutions encourage children to grow up fast and to look and behave like adults, but when these same young people become adolescents, they are sometimes expected to forget all that they have been through and to talk and to behave as children. The real stress of being pressured to grow up fast as a child is that it leaves the young person unprepared for the never-never land of adolescence.

SINGLE-PARENT FAMILIES AND CONTRACTS

Sociologist Erving Goffman of the University of Pennsylvania suggests that authority often exists as an "echelon" structure that has a natural hierarchy or chain of command. In two-parent families, the echelon structure is usually clear-cut: parents are in command and the children are subordinate. Parents decide which responsibilities warrant which freedoms, which achievements warrant which supports, and which loyalties warrant which commitments. In other words, much of the decision making is parental, even when the parents invite the participation of their offspring.[8]

In single-parent homes there is, of necessity, a breakdown in this echelon structure. This happens primarily because the effective exercise of authority requires some sort of support. In two-parent families, the parents usually support one another; they can discuss decisions, try out possible ideas, and so on. But in a single-parent family this is not possible; there is no one to work with who will provide support or encouragement.

It is not surprising, then, that many single parents turn to their children for support. In effect this means that contracts are rewritten so that children are full partners. This is a very common way in which children are hurried, and while it alone may not be overly stressful, combined with some of the other stresses young people are exposed to, it could be harmful.

The rewriting of a contract in single-parent homes is often in the freedom-responsibility domain. For example, children may become very involved in their parent's dating practices. If, say, the mother comes back very late and slightly high, the children may argue against her dating that particular man again. And if the parent brings a friend home to spend the night, children assess the respon-

136

sibility with which that delicate situation is handled before giving their blessing for a repeat of the event.

Children also begin to participate on equal terms in the achievement-support contract. A mother who takes on a new job after years of being at home raising her children may get considerable support from her children, who listen to her stories about her boss and co-workers and help out at home by doing some of the cleaning, cooking, and yard work. Children may also support the mother in her decisions to take courses, give up smoking, diet, and so on. In all these instances children begin to play the supportive role that would ordinarily be played by a marital partner.

Finally, the children may also participate on equal terms in the loyalty-commitment contract. That is, the single parent may begin to go out with men or women who might pose a threat of loyalty to the children. In the two-parent family, the loyalty of parents is taken for granted because the adults are the biological parents and this imposes a sort of automatic loyalty. The affection of one parent for the other is not seen as a threat to loyalty, since both parents are biologically bound to the children. But when, for example, the mother dates a man who has no biological relation to her children, he can pose a loyalty threat that the biological father never did. Because the new man has no biological bond to the children, the mother's attachment to him could be seen as a withdrawal of loyalty, whereas her attachment to the biological father would have been seen as evidence of loyalty.

Accordingly, in single-parent homes, parental loyalty cannot be taken for granted, and the children are in the position of giving commitment in return for parental loyalty. Adolescent children, for example, may offer to stay home or go to a movie with their mother if she is dating a man they do not like. In this instance the children are willing to show commitment, give of their time and energy to the mother's happiness, in return for a demonstration of loyalty to them.

Thus the children of single-parent homes are encouraged to grow up fast because they are, of necessity, put into a reciprocal role with respect to contracts. Allocating freedoms in response to demonstrations of responsibility, offering support in reaction to achievement, and showing commitment in return for loyalty are

adult functions. To operate in this way, the child has to try and behave like a knowledgeable adult. Children do not always succeed at
this, but in this situation they have some pressure to behave as a
parental partner, and this is pressure to grow up fast.

The normal process of aquiring reciprocal contracting skills
may be impaired in children who have been hurried, for these children are often "out of phase" with their peers. Because hurried children are, consciously or unconsciously, expected to be "ahead" of
their peers in intellectual or social skills, they are often competitive
and egocentric in their peer relationships. These young people may
adopt the adult unilateral approach to contracting to their peers.
For example, an attractive adolescent girl I know had been groomed
since childhood to be a physician. She met a young man she liked,
but the relationship did not last long. She expected him to take her
out regardless of whether he had to study or not, but if she had to
study, she would refuse to go out and would rebuke him for asking
her. This young woman, hurried since childhood, had no sense of the
reciprocity of contracts; she treated her peer as a child.

Young people who have been hurried often have trouble knowing which type of contracting is appropriate. In college, for example,
these young people may criticize a professor for such things as not
grading exams immediately, although they never get their own work
in on time. It is the professor's job to be responsible, not the students'. At work, such young people dislike being told what to do and
behave as if the employer is dependent on their support for his or
her achievement as much as the reverse. In marriage relationships,
where reciprocity must be present, such young people will often behave unilaterally and demand achievement (do the dishes, clean the
house) in return for support but without feeling that they have to re-
ciprocate in any way (pay the bills, take out the garbage).

Hurrying children is thus not only a violation of contracts but
can also impair the child's understanding of the appropriateness of
unilateral and reciprocal contracting. Hurried children may adopt
an authoritarian attitude with peers and friends where it is inappropriate, but not at school or work, where it is. It is because they have
difficulty knowing when to contract unilaterally or reciprocally that
hurried young people often seem to be rude and ill-mannered.

Understanding the structure of human relationships is essential to good manners. In French, the phrase *mal elevé* (badly brought up) is as bad an insult as can be leveled at a child. Unfortunately, many hurried children, because they seem to lack good manners, could be said to be *mal elevé*.

Chapter 7

Hurried Children: Stressed Children

S igmund Freud gave us our first comprehensive understanding of emotional illness. Disturbed human behavior that had once been attributed to the work of the devil could now be understood in entirely human terms. Basically, Freud argued, disturbed behavior arises out of conflict; it is a symptom of conflict either within the individual or between the individual and others. The "hysterical" woman, for example, who dresses and behaves provocatively but insists that men are always bothering her is in conflict over her sexuality. Unconsciously, she wants to attract men; consciously she does not. The treatment of such a problem, according to Freud, was to make the patient aware of her conflicted motives and in this way produce a resolution and a disappearance or diminution of the symptoms, namely, anxiety.[1]

Freud also suggested that the disturbed behavior of the neurotic or psychotic was an exaggeration of a normal reaction to conflict. We all have the potential to become neurotic or psychotic if we are faced with sufficient conflict. Indeed, animals have been made "neurotic" experimentally by presenting them with a situation where pain was the price of a reward. In one experiment, rats were trained to find food in a certain place, then the path to the food was electrified so the animals would be shocked en route. Animals in this situation, desiring to get the food but afraid to do so, showed many disturbed behaviors—they urinated, defecated, went around in circles, and moved toward the food and away from it again and again.

It is clear, then, that conflict is a major cause of emotional distress. And to the extent that hurrying causes conflict, which it often does, it is also a cause of distress. But some years ago Hans Selye, a neurophysiologist at McGill University in Montreal, identified a type of distress reaction that is common to everyone and which, while it may not produce neurotic or psychotic behavior, can have negative effects for the individual's psychic and physical well-being.[2]

Selye demonstrated that our bodies react in a stereotyped and specific way to any special or extra demand (physical, emotional, intellectual) made upon it. Selye speaks of situations, events or people who produce the stress reaction as "stressors." Stressors are not bad or good, they are just special demands. A passionate kiss, a large raise, a surprise victory, the success of a child are all stressors in the sense that they call for an extra effort of adaptation. In some ways our bodies are like machines—the more we use them, the sooner they wear out. Whether the machine is used for good or evil, to make guns or tractors, is not relevant. It is the *amount* of use to which the machine is put, not the purpose, that determines how quickly it will start to break down.

In effect, then, stress is the wear and tear on our bodies that is produced by the very process of living. When we say of someone, like the President, "How he has aged in the job," we are talking about a stress reaction. The special demands made upon a President are enormous and the effects are not neuroses or psychoses but, rather, premature aging. Clearly there are individual differences and some people don't wear out as quickly as others, but undue stress always hurries the aging process.

What Selye has done, therefore, is to make us look beyond conflict to understand human distress. The theory of conflict suggests that in the absence of conflict, life is smooth and harmonious. Emotional and physical health are predicated on the avoidance of debilitating intrapsychic or intrapersonal conflict. But we know that living itself is stressful and that a life without conflict is not a life without stress. Indeed conflict is just one, albeit a powerful, stressor.

It is my contention that the practice of hurrying children, in any of the ways described in the earlier chapters, is a stressor. Whether we are hurrying children from babysitter to nursery school, or to do well on tests, or to deal with issues such as adult problems of sexuality, we are putting children under stress. While no one of these

142

demands may overstress a child, the more hurrying demands are made on a child, the more likely it will be that the child will be overstressed.

STRESS AND THE STRESS RESPONSE

According to Selye, each of us has a certain amount of "adaptation energy" that allows us to deal with the contingencies of everyday life. Adaptation energy enables children to learn at school and adults to perform their duties at work. Ordinarily this energy reservoir is replenished each day by the ingestion of food and by sleep.[3]

There are wide individual differences in the energy reservoirs we are blessed with at birth. Research by Alexander Thomas and Stella Chess of New York University, for example, shows that even shortly after birth, infants with different temperament types can be distinguished. Some infants are very active and some are very phlegmatic. These individual differences persist throughout life. We all know people who never seem able to sit still, who make us edgy because of the restless energy they communicate. Other people always seem tired and need a lot of sleep.

We tend to organize our lives in keeping with our relative energy levels. Most jobs are geared to what is probably the average energy level that allows us to work for eight hours, to sleep for eight hours, and to eat, relax, and play for eight hours. Individuals with higher energy levels often take on additional work and seem to need less time for rest, food intake, and relaxation. Other people, with low adaptation-energy levels, find even the average workday too long.

Most of the time we organize our lives so that we do not totally exhaust our daily supply of adaptation energy by the time we go to sleep; we keep a certain amount in reserve just in case of emergencies. If the car breaks down on the way to work, or if the furnace goes out, or the boiler bursts, or a relative gets ill or dies suddenly, we need to call on our energy reserves to meet such situations, which go beyond our usual energy requirements.

It is our energy reserves that enable us to deal with acute situations that demand enormous energy output. The mother who lifts a car that has fallen off a jack and onto her child is a case in point, but there are many less dramatic examples. After a busy day we rush our child to the emergency room when he or she has stepped on a dirty nail. We wait for a doctor and an examination, suffer with our child through the pain of the antiseptic and the bandaging, then rush home to finish the day's chores of making dinner, cleaning house, and so on. In the course of everyday life we call upon our energy reserves a great deal.

Ordinarily, there is time in between emergencies to replenish our energy reservoirs. We may sleep for a few extra hours after stressful occasions and neglect some routine chores, or we may decide not to go to a movie or out to dinner but to stay home, which is less energy-consuming. Usually we are vaguely conscious of what we are doing. After a long and difficult day we are aware that we are near the end of our reserve energy and that we badly need to replenish our energy sources. Fatigue is our cue to low energy levels.

Stress, then, is any unusual demand for adaptation that forces us to call upon our energy reserves over and above that which we ordinarily expend and replenish in the course of a twenty-four-hour period. Although stress, or extraordinary demands for adaptation, can be of all kinds—accidents, breakdowns, being late, major decisions, major failures, successes, and so on—the response to stress is fairly specific and well documented. In other words, our bodies have a very specific way of calling upon and utilizing our energy reserves. Selye calls this the "stress response."

The stress response dates back to the earliest stages of human evolution, to our animal heritage. We in fact have two brains: an old brain, which regulates most of our bodily functions—heart rate, respiration, adrenalin levels in the blood, and so on—and a new brain which permits memory, perception, reasoning, and the like. The old brain was essential when humans were still hunter-gatherers and were dependent upon the immediate physical environment for sustenance. Early man was constantly engaged in fighting off predators and in protecting himself and his family from severe weather and disasters.

Humans used on such occasions what they inherited from their animal ancestors—the old brain. Walter Cannon, an American physiologist, first described the stress response initiated by the old brain. He suggested that when the old brain was activated beyond normal levels, it prepared the individual for "fight or flight": "If fear always paralyzed, it would result in danger of destruction. But fear and aggressive feelings, as anticipatory responses to critical situations make ready for action and have great survival value."[4]

The stress response, as described by Cannon and later by Selye, has four steps. The first is a rapid mobilization of energy reserves. Messages are sent from the old brain to the nervous system and a general alarm is sounded. Adrenalin is pumped into the blood, heart rate quickens, breathing becomes more rapid, the stomach and intestines stop digesting, blood pressure rises dramatically, and the senses become more acute and more attuned to every sight and sound. Hormonal activity of many different kinds is at work to increase our energy reserves.

Often we may not be aware of this mobilization until after the stress is gone. For example, I do a good deal of public speaking in the United States and Canada, and I usually don't feel self-conscious or anxious before a talk to a large group of people. After the talk, however, I feel tired and emotionally drained. I always prefer to eat after a lecture rather than before because I sense that my digestive processes work better after the stress of public speaking is over. Giving a talk before a large group of people is an extraordinary event and calls forth the stress response. The same is true in many situations. When we have barely escaped a serious accident in a car, we experience the emotional surge only after we have taken the preventive action.

Once the alarm system has sounded, the next step is a rapid increase in energy consumption. At such times, we draw up our energy reserves of which, according to Selye, there is only a finite amount. The burning up of new energy as a response to stress helps to explain why some people lose weight when they are anxious or under pressure, even though they may be eating and drinking more than usual. Anxiety and worry burn up energy. Of course, some people overcompensate for the energy depletion caused by stress, and overeat. Paradoxically, both underweight and obesity can be direct or indirect responses to the body's rapid utilization of energy under stress.

The next step, for which the mobilization and energy consumption were preparatory, is vigorous physical activity of the sort that was essential to our ancestors' survival. They either had to run away quickly or engage in combat. In either case, our sensory motor system is ready for quick action. This preparation is still useful in some situations today. If you have ever had to rush someone to the hospital, run away from a vicious dog, or swim a long distance to assist someone in trouble in the water, you can really appreciate the mobilization for action provided by the stress response.

The last and final step in the stress reaction is a return to equilibrium. After a stressful situation, the usual reaction is to find peace and quiet. After a lecture to a large audience and a vigorous question-and-answer period, I just want to sit quietly. In the same way, someone who has had to work an extra shift, console grieved relatives, or deal with an angry customer needs some time to restore equilibrium and replenish energy reserves.

Although the stress response is clearly adaptive in many situations today, in many others it is not. For example, the motor action that we need to employ in steering to avoid an oncoming car in the wrong lane is far less than what we are prepared for by the stress response. Indeed the stress response may often be maladaptive in today's world. Consider a young man who had been told in front of the whole class, "Can't you do anything right?" His face flushed, his body tensed, his palms began to sweat, and he wanted in the worst way to run from the room. But he couldn't, because that would only confound the felony. He continued to sit in his chair beneath the snickering stares of his classmates. He didn't run but his head began to ache and his stomach felt distended; he was swallowing air in huge gulps. I know the reaction well because the young man was myself.

What happens if the stress response is elicited but the mobilization for action is prevented from running its course? The whole pattern of the stress response is interrupted, and equilibrium is restored not by the expenditure of energy through the musculature but rather by its dissipation in other body systems. Headaches, for example, are produced by constriction of blood vessels in the head. When we are stressed and our bodies are ready to take physical action, even the tiny muscles of the blood vessels contract so as to use up some of the mobilized energy. Selye describes the response to unrelieved stress reactions as "stress diseases." These diseases include hypertension, peptic ulcers, headaches, and heart disease.

When the stress diseases were first identified it was assumed that they were simply a direct reaction to unrelieved stress. But in recent years it has become clear that the relationship between stress and stress diseases is a fairly complicated one and that some intuitive assumptions need to be seriously examined. Consider a study of air traffic controllers, who track incoming and outgoing planes and must make instant decisions involving hundreds of lives:

> *Air traffic controllers, according to a classic study, track planes with their blood pressure; as the skies grow crowded, their arteries constrict and their blood pressure shoots up as much as 50 points. Their glands also squirt more of the nerve-stimulating chemical epinephrine, presenting a textbook picture of psychological stress. It goes without saying that the controllers develop a range of stress-related diseases and die of strokes by the age of 50 . . . except that they don't. On the contrary, the study found, by some measures the controllers are actually healthier than the rest of the population.*[5]

Research is just beginning to indicate that objective stress, such as that faced by air controllers, is only one of many factors that determine how individuals respond to stress. Just as important as the objective stress that air controllers face is their attitude toward stress and their strategies for dealing with it. In one study it was found that air controllers who were dissatisfied with their jobs were more at risk for stress-related diseases than were air controllers who were happy at their jobs. How we perceive stressful situations is apparently as important to our well-being as the objective stress situation itself.

Another example of incorrect inferences about the relation of stress to disease is the case of women at work. Conventional wisdom says that as women increasingly take on what were once considered male jobs, they become increasingly susceptible to the diseases of stress usually experienced by males. Recent issues of women's magazines are replete with articles about what the New York *Daily News* labeled "Lib Sickness." Even Hans Selye has written that "the more women assume male jobs, the more women are subject to so-called male diseases, such as cardiac infarction, gastric ulcers and hypertension. They get the same satisfactions too, of course, but at a price."[6]

But reporter Barbara Ehrenreich began looking for the data that indicated an increase in women's death rates from heart disease and other stress-related diseases. Although many professionals quoted such statistics, Ehrenreich could not track down any reference for them. When she asked a physician who had written a book on women's stress about his sources, he said: "I don't believe in statistics. Women have more love problems than men and now they have more work problems too. That is why they are dying."[7]

In fact, death rates for coronary heart disease, for example, are declining for both males and females, but the rate for females is declining faster than the rate for males. In 1960, males were 1.62 times as likely to die of coronary heart disease as females. In 1976, males were 2.1 times more likely to die of heart disease than women. Ehrenreich concludes:

> *The story on gender and longevity has not changed since the 1920s. Despite women's continuing influx into the work force, despite the "lifestyle" upheaval of the sixties and seventies (and it should be said—despite all the unnecessary surgery performed on women, the reckless prescribing of estrogens and other hazardous drugs and devices) women live longer than men and the gap continues to widen.*[8]

What does seem to matter is the attitude of women toward their work or home. An eight-year study of 900 women in Framingham, Massachusetts found that women who worked outside the home for more than half their adult lives were not significantly more likely to have developed heart disease than women who had remained at home. What seems to be stressful is not working or staying at home but rather the person's attitude toward these choices. A woman who has to work but would prefer to stay home is under more stress than a woman who prefers to work. In the same way, a woman who stays home when she would prefer to work is under more stress than the woman who prefers not to work and doesn't have to. Thus both work *and* staying home can be stressful if the woman is unhappy.

We cannot determine just from the objective amount of stress a person is under what his or her reaction to that stress may be. We need to know something about the person and about the stress situation before we can predict how the stress will affect the individual. The same is true for children, and we will now look at some of the basic types of stress that have been identified as affecting children and suggest how hurrying can promote or exacerbate these forms of stress.

STRESSED CHILDREN

Janet is ten years old but has many adult responsibilities. In addition to taking care of her clothes and room, she must prepare breakfast for herself and her younger sister and make sure that they get off to school on time. (Her mother leaves for work an hour before Janet needs to get to school). When she gets home, she has to do some housecleaning, defrost some meat for dinner, and make sure her sister is all right. When her mother gets home Janet listens patiently to her mother's description of the "creeps" at work who never leave her alone and who are always making cracks or passes. After Janet helps prepare dinner, her mother says, "Honey, will you do the dishes? I'm just too tired," and Janet barely has time to do some homework.

Children like Janet (and there are many of them) are stressed by responsibility overload. It is not just that Janet has a lot of work to do, for most children today could probably do more than they are required to do. In previous generations, the children of immigrants worked long, hard hours and nevertheless became competent, productive, and sound adults. What is really stressful in Janet's case is not the work but the responsibility the work entails. Janet feels responsible for her little sister, for her mother, for the house. This is really what distinguishes the hard-working children today from the immigrant children of previous generations. In the newly arrived families there was usually a mother and a father so that children did not have *parental* responsibilities. But in the one-parent home of today, children have to assume parental responsibilities. Such responsibilities are a lot for young people to carry and forces them to call again and again upon adaptation energy reserves.

Now consider Peter, a boy four years old. Both his mother and father work and they have enrolled him in a full-day private nursery. In addition, because both parents have to leave home early, they have arranged to leave Peter with a neighbor, who will prepare him for the car pool person, who will take him to school before nine o'clock. After school, the car pool person drops him off at the neighbor's house again until his parents come to pick him up after work. By the time he gets home, Peter has been out of the house for almost twelve hours and has adapted to a number of different places (neighbor's house, car, school) and a number of different people (neighbor, car pool person, teachers).

This is a lot of adaptation for a four-year-old, and he has had to call upon his energy reserves in order to cope. Is it really surprising that his teachers complain that he is whining and fussy, that he does not seem interested in playing with the other children, and that he sometimes sits quietly staring into space while touching two blocks together, back and forth, back and forth? Peter is clearly at the limit of his energy reserves. He suffers from change overload.

Emotional overload can occur as well as responsibility and change overload. When, for example, children overhear parents quarreling, they are not only upset by the negative emotions but also by what is being said. Threats made in anger to a spouse are often branded upon the child's psyche even when the child cannot really understand their full import. As one four-year-old said to his father some months after overhearing a particularly violent quarrel, "Are you really going to take a job out West and find a woman who appreciates a man who brings home a steady pay check?" The child knew the threat by heart, adult words and all—he carried it with him as a continual source of stress.

Of course, parents have always quarreled and children have heard such quarrels. But it is much more common today since parents are encouraged to "let it all hang out" and even to learn how to fight in a productive way. In his book *Intimate Enemies*, George Bach provides rules for couples doing battle with one another.[9] In addition, because more and more workers are engaged in service or white-collar activities, there are more people who lack physical avenues for "letting off the steam" (the old-fashioned term for the stress response) generated at work. Unlike the laborer, the white-collar worker has no physical outlet for stress and often brings it home. Quarreling, complaining, and bickering between husband and wife stresses children by overloading them with fears and anxieties for which they may have no outlet.

Emotional overload is also produced by separation of any kind—being left with a baby sitter, going to nursery or public school, going away to a camp for a couple of weeks, business travel of a parent, parental divorce or death—is stressful. Separation is a normal and healthy part of growth and no child can, or should be, spared the pain of separation. But too much separation can over-stress a child and lead to symptoms of stress disease. It is not separation per se but too much separation too soon that is stressful and harmful to children.

Children today experience separation most frequently in con-nection with the divorce of parents. Divorce hurries children be-cause it forces them to deal with separations that, in the usual course of events, they would not have to deal with until adolescence or young adulthood. Divorce and separation are painful even when parents take care to prepare children for the rupture and if they co-operate in the child care and do not use the children as weapons against one another. Although children under such circumstances usually cope quite well, there is always some pain and confusion about what is happening and why it is happening.

When separation is not handled well, the stress for children is considerable. Separation may entail a move to a new house or apart-ment, new friends, or a new school. In addition, the family's eco-nomic situation can be dramatically different with much less money to spend; children may have to take on new responsibilities for self and home care. And the child may be torn between mother and father, each of whom is trying to win the child away from the other. This is the real loss of innocence: losing the implicit belief that the world is a good and stable place in which to live—that the family, the child's basic source of security, will always be there. A child who witnesses the dissolution of a family must of necessity grow up fast and face stresses that are not usually encountered until a later age.

The stress on a child of separation from the father (the most usual parent to leave in a divorce) has only come to be appreciated fully in the last fifteen years. It was once thought that a father's ab-sence was not stressful to children, that fathers were really not im-portant in a child's upbringing. In an official report issued by the World Health Organization in 1951, child psychiatrist John Bowlby—the first to highlight the stress of separation from a loved one as a serious health risk—wrote that the father is "of no direct importance to the young child, but is of indirect value as economic support and in his emotional support of the mother."[10] Even the late

Margaret Mead expressed the same attitude when she quipped that "a father is a biological necessity but a social accident."

This attitude toward fathers was reflected in comic strips such as "Dagwood Bumstead," whose adventures involved his bathtub, his boss, his neighbor, or some traveling salesman. He was rarely seen interacting with his own children. Usually Blondie intervened. And the one child who did interact with him, a paperboy, often won out in the confrontation.

In the past decade or so, however, we have come to understand how much even young children are attached to their fathers and how important this attachment is for healthy growth and development. In part this may be because contemporary fathers are likely to be more involved in child care than in the past and to feel more comfortable in the nurturant role. But fathers were probably always more important to children than was thought in the past. Separation from the father as a result of divorce is an emotional overload and is a powerful stressor to children.

The potency of separation as a stressor is evidenced by the fact that today—because divorce is so common—children from two-parent families are stressed by the very possibility of divorce. The following conversation gives evidence of this concern.

"Daddy, when are you and Mommy getting divorced?" My five-year-old son asked this question nonchalantly as I drove him to school on a Tuesday morning not long ago. I was stunned and a little panicked by the question, and I tried desparately to recall if Ann and I had been bickering lately.

"What do you mean?" I asked, in a tone of syrupy solicitousness that grown-ups often inflict upon kids. "Mommy and Daddy haven't been fighting, have we?"

"No," he allowed, cheerful. "But everybody gets divorced."

"No, no, not everybody," I said. "Lots of Mommies and Daddies stay married all their lives."

"Oh yeah, what about Jason? and Tommy? and Lisa?" He rattled off the names of a dozen or so of his playmates and classmates, all of them children of divorced parents. "And what about Grandpa and Grandma. They were divorced, weren't they?"

> *"Well, yes." I was caught in the withering cross fire that kids often inflict upon grown-ups. "But your Mommy and Daddy are never going to get divorced. So don't worry about it, okay?"*
>
> *"Okay." He was satisfied and moved on to more urgent concerns. "Can we go to McDonald's for dinner tonight?"*[11]

Divorce and the threat of divorce are not the only separation fears children have to deal with. Modern jet travel has created a new breed of traveling business men (and, increasingly, business women) who spend as much time on the road as they do at home. The following anecdote illustrates the kind of stress this separation can produce.

> *It is Mark's seventh birthday. His school friends are gathered at the house for Sunday lunch and it's time to blow out the candles, cut the cake and open the presents. The room is filled with noise and laughter. The parents of some of Mark's friends line the room, their faces beaming with delight. One figure, however, is glaringly absent, Mark's father. He is 1,500 miles away on a business trip.*
>
> *Mark's father, vice president of an industrial consulting firm, spends nearly a third of his life "on the road." When family togetherness is natural and precious—on holidays, the days of school performances, birthdays, the little league championship game—Dad is likely to be elsewhere: in a hotel room, conference hall or taxi.*[12]

Separation from parents as a result of divorce or travel—or imagined separation—can overload children emotionally with distress, fears (that the parent will never return), and anxieties (maybe the child caused the parent to leave). Parents are the most important people in the world to their children and separation is a very powerful stressor.

STRESSES OF SCHOOLING

Schools today stress children in a variety of ways quite beyond the familiar stress of competition for grades and honors. For example, schools are much more a host to theft and violence than ever before. Likewise, schools tend to stereotype children and impose false expectancies upon them. Finally, students are increasingly taught in environments that impede effective learning. These features of schooling force children to deal with adult issues and ineptitudes at an early age and hence are stressful pressures to grow up fast.

Not long ago a sixth grader, who lives in the affluent suburb of Lexington, Massachusetts, and I were talking about his going to junior high school the next year. I was curious about his feelings —whether or not he was looking forward to it. Although he was a good student and well liked by his peers, he seemed unenthusiastic about junior high. I wondered whether this was because he would no longer be with his friends, or because he would be in the youngest (least powerful) group rather than the oldest. But his lack of enthusiasm was eventually expressed in a rather unexpected way: "I don't want to get beat up," he said.

What this young man, and many of his friends, feared about junior high were the "druggies" he had heard hang out there. Stories of getting held up or getting beat up are rife among young people and constitute an ironic fear of growing up too fast just when many societal pressures are pushing children in that direction. Unfortunately, young people's fears are not unfounded and too many teenagers have discovered the hazards of leaving a bike unlocked or a watch or clothing unattended.

The following comment was made to David Owen, a writer posing as a student in Bingham High School, serving working- and middle-class families. It was made by a male student about the "hoods" in his school.

"They're *tough* mothers," Bill says. "Those guys don't think twice about stomping on you if you get in their way."

Reporter Owen comments: "Bill's anxiety about hoods is the main reason it's taking us so long to get to our lunch. The food line is generally known as the Hood Line, and Bill doesn't want to take chances. Most of the guys in the Hood Line are about six feet tall and 180 pounds. They're all wearing leather jackets and seven-pound motorcycle boots. In their back pockets are oversized black leather wallets that hook onto their belts with metal chains. Not exactly the kind of guys who would lend you a dime for chocolate milk."[13]

Although there are no reliable statistics about the incidence of violence or theft among young people, the statistics with respect to teachers are revealing. If young people are not afraid of attacking or stealing from teachers, they are certainly not going to be afraid of attacking or stealing from peers. According to the National Education Association (NEA), assaults against teachers are increasing. And the same is true for acts of theft and vandalism with teachers as targets.

According to a 1979 NEA survey some 110,000 teachers—one out of every twenty—were physically attacked by students on school property during the 1978–79 school year. Another 10,000 were attacked by students off school property. The 110,000 victims represent an increase of 57 percent over the estimated 70,000 teachers who were attacked during 1977–78. Of the teachers who were attacked, an estimated 11,500 required medical attention for physical injuries and an estimated 9,000 required medical attention for emotional trauma.

Ten percent of all respondents thought it likely that they would be physically attacked sometime in the near future. Teachers in the northeast, in the inner city, and in large school systems expressed this fear more often than teachers generally. In addition to fears of physical attacks, about one fourth of respondents reported that they had had personal property stolen during 1978–79 and about the same proportion said that personal property had been damaged at school.[14]

The figures for assault and theft from children at or around schools are, at the very least, comparable to those experienced by teachers. In Cambridge, Massachusetts, a black student was killed in the high school, a finale to escalating confrontations. Many high schools now employ scanners, like those at airports, to ensure that students are not entering classrooms with concealed weapons. These problems are not just with inner city schools but occur as well in affluent suburbs and in small towns.

What all this means is that young peoople today are hurried by their schools into attitudes of wariness and fear, which have no place in school where children's major energies need to be directed toward learning. Indeed, one of the issues not addressed by the current management systems approach to schools is the level of violence and crime that of necessity touches all pupils. Could it be that at least some school failure is attributable to the fear of personal injury engendered by the educational experience?

Schools also hurry and stress children when the teachers and administrators operate on the basis of *stereotypes* and *false expectancies*, which place children in fixed compartments of behavior and thought that are often alien to the child's own inclinations. Stereotyping and false expectancies are particularly common with respect to children of separation and divorce, a growing segment of all school populations.

Teachers and administrators, for example, frequently expect that a child from a divorced family is going to have problems. Likewise, any difficulty the child does encounter is immediately attributed to the family problem without any consideration of possible other problems such as, say, poor vision.

As John Orth, principal of Oak Terrace High School in Highwood, Illinois, writes:

> *When families face a crisis there is a great deal the school can do to help without usurping traditional parental prerogatives.... The most important one, in my belief, is also the most basic and that is to re-examine our own attitudes and how they come across to the children in our care. Do we, in our own minds, attach a stigma to separation and divorce? Do we automatically expect the worst when we learn that a child's parents have separated? Are we sensitive to the signs, many of them subtle, that signal real confusion and stress in a child? Do we recognize and openly acknowledge the strength and independence many children develop when they learn to cope with that confusion and stress?*[15]

Schools also hurry children by labelling children too quickly and too early for management rather than pedagogical reasons. Sometimes such labelling and its consequences for the children involved come close to being criminal. Many young children, for example, are diagnosed as learning disabled or retarded when in fact they may have limited vision or hearing or come from a bilingual home and have limited command of English. It is much easier for teachers and administrators to label such children and to relegate them to some special program than to deal with their special needs.

156

Our language is really of little help in this regard because it reverses the true order of things and puts the adjective before the noun—retarded child rather than a child with retardation. Branded and put into special classes early, many children decide, "If you have the name, you might as well play the game," and become what they are expected to be: retarded, learning disabled, or whatever.

Schools stress children in other ways that have recently been enumerated by writer Leslie A. Hart:

- *The classroom size is the wrong size for all activities except rote—too small for films, lectures, and visitors; too large for discussions, projects and the like . . .*
- *The classroom day involves thousands of events and interactions. Rarely is a teacher activity continuous for as long as two minutes. Disciplinary remarks and actions may take more time than instruction. Seldom can teachers have a one-on-one talk with a student that exceeds thirty seconds. In actuality none of the individualizing that gets talked about happens: simply putting a child into a different group may be called individualizing.*
- *Little time is given to actual instruction in classrooms. Management, busywork, waiting, leaving and arriving, and other diversions reduce gross instructional time to around ninety minutes a day. . . . In class, attention to single students may average, per student, only six hours per year.*
- *To "cover the material," teachers need response from students able and willing to give it, and so they pay attention to about a third of the class, largely ignoring those who need instruction most, who may be written off as "failures" in the early weeks of the semester. A high percentage of failure is expected and accepted.* [16]

Such practices hurry children both in a clock and in a calendar sense. They hurry children by rushing them from one subject or activity to another. Children thus never have a sense of completion and this is stressful. Children who learn at school often do so despite, rather than because of, educational practice. This practice hurries children in the calendar sense by pushing them into adult attitudes of resignation about the inadequacies, rigidities, and un-changeability of "the system."

School can also stress children because it is so tedious. One of the stresses that contributes to job burnout among adults is work that is repetitious and meaningless. Boredom can sometimes be much more stressful than excitement. A bored person often feels un-happy and trapped, and this brings on the stress reaction. But workers in repetitious, meaningless jobs have no safety valves for their stress reaction and so they become fatigued, inattentive, and careless. The result is that they often lose, or quit, their jobs.

For many young people school represents a boring, meaningless activity. In this respect schools hurry children by pushing them into the dull routines of much adult work. A sensitive portrayal of this sort of academic boredom and stress was provided by a young man interviewed by Thomas Cottle. The young man is "Bobby" Hardwicke, who attends a private school in the suburbs of Hartford, Connecticut, and has parents who are professionals. Bobby says:

> *No one likes to recognize what people like me have to go through. I'm sure if you asked most people they'd say the life of a teenager is a dream. Everyone I talk to seems to want to be young again, which is one of the sicknesses of the culture. We've discussed this in school many times. But no one sees us for what we are. First off, teenagers or what-ever you want to call us, are people. Real, live people. I know that sounds strange, but you can't believe how many times I'm treated like a thing. In stores, or the post offices, I'm this one's son, that one's classmate, that one's student.*
>
> *I'll go to college, although I think now the best thing for me would be to take a year out and work somewhere. I've never really worked—at something real, I mean. Something that would make the slightest difference to somebody. I've studied Latin for two years, all right. I get A's. I get A's in History, European History. Okay, so I've done well, although I think anybody could do well at this place if they were half-way verbal. All the classes are small and we don't have that many exams, so all you have to do,*

like we always kid each other, is talk good. "I talk good,
Mrs. Arnold, so can I get a good grade now?"

So with all the studying and talking good, you know
what I'd really like to do? Carpentry. I'd like to build a
house, or fix someone's stairs or porch. Something real.

You know what it is? You go to a school like this, it
costs a lot of money, a whole lot in fact, and all you think
about is doing well so you can get into a good college, and
because just going to college doesn't mean a thing, you ask
yourself, "What am I doing? What does any of this matter!"
And the answer is, it doesn't matter at all. One course is
only meant to get you to the next one and then the one after
that and not one of it makes the slightest bit of difference
until you are all done. So you can look back and say, "Well
I did it, I passed; so now what?" All school is, you know, is
the great time passer. It's a big invention to keep kids from
becoming anything.[17]

School can stress children by hurrying them into dealing with
threats of violence and crime; into stereotyped roles and attitudes;
and into boring, no-end, meaningless activities. Schools thus, often
add to rather than subtract from the stress experienced by children
in contemporary society.

MEDIA AND STRESS

As we have seen, contemporary media hurry children in one of two
different ways; they may give children too much information too
fast or they may give young people information that is too complex
or abstract for children to understand. The first kind of hurrying
produces the stress of information overload, the second produces
the stress of emotional overload.

Ordinarily, children have ways of resisting information overload. Once, for example, I took my three sons who were four, six,
and nine years old at the time, to a three-ring circus. I bought good
seats in anticipation of my sons' delight at what I remembered with
such good feelings. But once the show began, I was dismayed that
the boys were not watching. "Look at that lady in the pink dress on

the elephant," I said, or "Look at that man on the bike on the tight-rope." But the boys were paying attention to only one thing, namely, the vendors selling hot dogs, cold drinks, peanuts, and cotton candy. My boys seemed more excited about eating than about watching the show. I told myself that I had learned a lesson, never again.

Some weeks later, however, much to my surprise, the boys spontaneously began to discuss the circus at the dinner table. "Boy did you see the lady in the pink dress on the elephant!" exclaimed Ricky. "How did she manage to stay on with just one foot?" Then Bobby piped in, "Yeh and that guy on the bike on the tightrope was pretty neat too, I'd like to try that." And so it went; the boys had enjoyed the circus but there was just too much information to deal with all at once, and they needed time to digest it.

Television, in particular, does not permit time for digestion of information overload. Because children watch television every day, there is little time for reflection. And, because television is in the home and is a shared experience, it is more a natural experience than the contrived experience of the circus. Children handle the overload by tuning in and out or by using television as a backdrop for play, homework, or practicing the guitar.

Accordingly, it is probably the form of television, its omnipresence as an information conveyer, that may be as stressful or more stressful than the content per se. Television forces children to accommodate a great deal and inhibits the assimilation of material. Consequently, the television child knows a great deal more than he or she can ever understand. This discrepancy between how much information children have and what they can process is the major stress of television.

Perhaps this is why Marshall McLuhan writes: "The television generation is a grim bunch. It is much more serious than children of any other period—when they were frivolous, more whimsical. The television child is more earnest, more dedicated."[18]

In a sense, because children constantly have to accommodate to the information provided by television, they work more and play less. And play, as we shall see, is an important stress valve. Ironically, one way television hurries children is by depriving them of time for play and hence for relieving stress.

The media also stress children by presenting them with material that is too complex or abstract for them to deal with. Sometimes when children are confronted with difficult concepts and ideas, as in programs like *NOVA*, the struggle to understand can be intellectually stimulating. But there is much on television, and in some books and movies, that is puzzling to children but that is not intellectually stimulating. Indeed, much of the sexual and violent material can have a disturbing and stressful effect.

Children are not fully secure in who they are, what their roles are. Even teenagers are not yet fully comfortable with their sexuality, or with their angers and hostilities. When children see angry outbursts, rape, or violent attacks on television, it is stressful because it portrays adults who have no control over the impulses the young person is struggling to master. Presenting children with adult material is stressful because it suggests that maybe they will not be able to master their impulses and hostilities.

This, by the way, is quite a different issue from a child's modeling of the violence he or she sees on television. Modelling is not in question here; emotional maturity is. Adults who have considerable experience with their emotions and impulses can usually view those who have lost control with some degree of distance. But loss of control can be threatening even to adults. With children, in whom controls are just developing, the observation of adults who have lost control or who are viciously deviant can be a powerful stressor, as it suggests that they may not gain control either.

Thus media stress children by giving them too much information too fast or by giving them information for which they are not intellectually or emotionally ready.

A STRESS TEST FOR CHILDREN

Children, then, are stressed by a wide variety of incidents—some positive, others benign, many negative. Like the many adult stress tests given today, we can chart a child's stress level by assessing the stressors he or she has undergone recently. The following scale gives an estimate of the impact of various changes in a child's life that hurry and stress them. Add up the total points for all of the items your child has experienced in the last year. If your child scored below 150, he or she is about average with respect to stress load. If your child's score was between 150 and 300 he or she has a better than average chance of showing some symptoms of stress. If your child's score was above 300 there is a strong likelihood he or she will experience a serious change in health and/or behavior.[19]

Stress	Points	Child's Score
Parent dies	100	
Parents divorce	73	
Parents separate	65	
Parent travels as part of job	63	
Close family member dies	63	
Personal illness or injury	53	
Parent remarries	50	
Parent fired from job	47	
Parents reconcile	45	
Mother goes to work	45	
Change in health of a family member	44	
Mother becomes pregnant	40	
School difficulties	39	
Birth of a sibling	39	
School readjustment (new teacher or class)	39	
Change in family's financial condition	38	
Injury or illness of a close friend	37	
Starts a new (or changes) an extracurricular activity (music lessons, Brownies, and so forth)	36	
Change in number of fights with siblings	35	
Threatened by violence at school	31	
Theft of personal possessions	30	
Changes responsibilities at home	29	
Older brother or sister leaves home	29	
Trouble with grandparents	29	
Outstanding personal achievement	28	
Move to another city	26	
Move to another part of town	26	
Receives or loses a pet	25	
Changes personal habits	24	
Trouble with teacher	24	
Change in hours with baby sitter or at day-care center	20	

Stress	Points	Child's Score
Move to a new house	20	
Changes to a new school	20	
Changes play habits	19	
Vacations with family	19	
Changes friends	18	
Attends summer camp	17	
Changes sleeping habits	16	
Change in number of family get-togethers	15	
Changes eating habits	15	
Changes amount of TV viewing	13	
Birthday party	12	
Punished for not "telling the truth"	11	

Chapter 8

How Children React to Stress

*H*ow children respond to chronic stress depends upon several different factors, including the child's perception of the stress situation, the amount of stress he or she is under, and the availability of effective coping mechanisms. Thus how children respond to chronic stress is in part an individual matter. "The boiling water that hardens the egg softens the carrot" is but one of many proverbs that speaks to the fact that the stress that will cause one person to fall apart will strengthen another person's resolve— "when the going gets tough, the tough get going."

It is not always easy to predict how a particular child will respond to stress. Sometimes children surprise you. I have seen a rather clingy, dependent boy become quite independent and self-sufficient when this was demanded of him. And I have seen another young man who was doing well at school and at home despite a mother who had deserted and a father who was alcoholic. But when some boys threatened this young man while he was doing his paper route and took the money he had collected, he went into hysterics and had to be hospitalized.

FREE-FLOATING ANXIETY

For some children, chronic stress is translated into what Freud called "free-floating anxiety" in the sense that it is not attached to a specific fear or apprehension. The child feels restless, irritable, and unable to concentrate but is not really sure what the trouble is. One often sees such free-floating anxiety in children whose parents have just separated. Children at such times really don't know what to expect, and it is simply not knowing what to be afraid of that produces free-floating anxiety. Here are a couple of examples:

> *For most of an hour, Saul angrily protested the excessive demands being made upon him by his sixth grade teacher. "How can he expect me to do all this work when I'm so busy thinking of the divorce? It's not fair." Normally a good student, Saul was unable to finish assignments or prepare for tests. When he was admonished for incomplete work, he sullenly fled the classroom. Had he explained his distress to his teacher? "No," said Saul, "my teacher wouldn't understand, he doesn't even care, he just wants my work." Saul's distressed and angry preoccupation with his parents' divorce had interfered with his ability to concentrate and now everything seemed to be falling apart.*
>
> *Carol's second grade teacher reported that the girl seemed relieved "lighter, more carefree" after her parents' separation. Then, two months later, Carol began to whine and cry often begging for her classmates' possessions. "She eats her lunch at 10:00 in the morning," said the teacher, "then she pleads for more food at lunchtime because she has nothing left." Carol told her teacher she no longer cared about her school work and didn't want to help anymore in the classroom. In fact, she said fearfully, "I don't want to do anything."[1]*

These examples were taken from a five-year study of 131 children, of ages three to eighteen, who had experienced separation and divorce. As suggested in the examples above, more than 90 percent of the children experienced the divorce as extraordinarily stressful. Two concerns seemed to dominate their thinking: Who will take care of me (protect me, feed me, love me)? Will my relationship with my mother and father last? At all age levels, youngsters felt that they now "faced a world that was suddenly less reliable, less likely to be concerned with future hopes and needs. Their preoccupation with the newly felt unpredictability of life invaded much of their thinking and attention. Many of the children displayed a sadness and yearning for the family as it was and were unhappy with the amount of time they were spending with the father (when the mother had custody). Most of the children also harbored the wish that their parents would be reconciled. Such wishes persisted alongside a clear intellectual understanding that the divorce was final. Another characteristic revealed by the study was an increase in aggressive behavior. The children were more irritable, more given to losing their temper, more aggressive (pushing and shoving) toward peers and siblings than they had been before.[2]

Other studies also give evidence that the free-floating anxiety associated with the stress of separation and divorce affects children's school behavior. A recent large-scale study of almost twenty thousand children, both elementary and secondary pupils, from all over the country determined that certain general trends distinguished children from one-parent homes and those from two-parent homes.[3] For example, children from one-parent homes were lower in school achievement and had more tardies and absences than did children from two-parent homes. Likewise, children from one-parent homes visited the health clinic more, had more referrals for discipline, and were suspended more often than children from two-parent homes. These findings suggest the many different ways that the free-floating anxiety associated with the stress of separation and divorce appears in children's school behavior. However, remember that these are averages and do not hold for every child who has experienced separation and divorce.

Separation is perhaps the major factor in the free-floating anxiety of children of divorce but it is not the only one. Other events related to divorce can unduly stress children and leave them anxious and unsettled. For instance, an increasing number of children are kidnapped and retained by the noncustodial parent. It has been estimated that some 100,000 children are snatched by mothers and fathers each year, and about one-fifth are found. The stress on a kidnapped child is enormous. Constantly on the move, with a parent anxious about being found out, children are without consistent schooling and peer friendships. Such children are forced to grow up fast, and those who are eventually returned show many stress symptoms, usually free-floating anxiety. The following case is illustrative:

> *In January 1979, James Kennedy was kidnapped by his father. In March 1981, an alert schoolteacher, responding to a picture of James that was published in the* Ladies Home Journal, *reported to the authorities. When James*

was returned to his mother, he was quiet and fearful whereas before he had been outgoing. The two and a half years he spent with his father are still a mystery. Pat Kennedy, James's mother, knows that "James lived in Florida, Massachusetts, Tennessee, Connecticut and Pennsylvania, and stayed for short times in Vermont and New Hampshire. He was enrolled in five or six schools at least and at one point was left for several months with one of his father's acquaintances."

"He was obviously a very lonely little boy, very forlorn," says the teacher who called Pat from Pennsylvania. "Once I saw his father carrying him through a crowded hallway at school by the back of his collar and belt, and he just flung Jimmy into the classroom so that he landed on the floor. The boy was crying pretty hard, and I just knew there was something wrong with the way things were at home."

Once back with his mother, James has settled into a more routine existence, but evidence of free-floating anxiety persists.

"He seems a normal, endearing little boy—except that even now his life is far from normal. You can tell from the way he jumps when he hears a noise outside that the fear is still there. . . . The fear of being snatched again."[4]

In addition to the stresses associated with divorce, contemporary children may be stressed into free-floating anxiety by films or television programs that the children are not emotionally prepared to handle. Free-floating anxiety is also common among young children who are hurried from baby sitter to day-care center to baby sitter. Free-floating anxiety in the form of restlessness, irritability, inability to concentrate, and low mood is perhaps the most pervasive immediate response children exhibit to the stress of hurrying.

And all the signs point to a large increase in this syndrome. Pediatricians are reporting an increase in children with stomachaches and headaches that appear to be stress related. In adolescents, free-floating anxiety can take the form of depression and contribute to suicide. In Toronto, as in many large cities, the increases in stress reactions among young people have been so great that special child and adolescent services have been set up to care for these youngsters. Clinical psychologist Diane Syer, on the staff of the crisis intervention unit at Toronto East General Hospital, says this trend can be blamed on the fragmentation of the family and the erosion of social institutions such as religion, the mobility of people in our society, and a pervasive sense that the future will be grim.[5]

TYPE A BEHAVIOR

It has long been known that some adults cope with stress with a characteristic personality pattern. This pattern includes competitive achievement, striving, impatience, and aggression, both verbal and physical. Such personalities can be identified either by clinical interview or by a questionnaire. Another type of personality, Type B, is defined by the absence of Type A characteristics. The significance of the Type A personality is that persons who manifest it are twice as likely to develop coronary heart disease as Type B persons.

In the last few years investigators have been able to identify children with Type A and Type B personalities. In one investigation, for example, it was found that Type A children responded to stress in a manner comparable to Type A adults. That is, when Type A children and adults feel they are losing control of a situation that really matters to them, they make vigorous efforts to maintain control. The two personality types do not differ in their behavior, however, when they perceive that they are in complete control of the situation. Type A characteristics are brought out in response to a perceived loss of control over a significant situation.[6]

The significance of these findings has recently been made clear by Dr. Gerald Berenson and his colleagues at Louisiana State University, who examined 378 children of ages two to seventeen in Franklinton, Louisiana. This is but part of a larger sample of a long-term study of some 6,000 to 7,000 Louisiana youngsters. The aim of the study was to determine whether Type A behavior in children had the same physiological correlates that seem to predispose Type A adults to coronary heart disease. The results were as expected— Type A children had more cholesterol in their bloodstreams than did Type B children. The investigators conclude: "It is highly probable that certain personality and behavior traits (competitiveness, overeating, restlessness) that occur in children influence the early development of coronary artery disease and essential hypertension." Responding to the results of the Louisiana study, Dr. W. B. Kannel, a noted investigator of Type A behavior in adults, said that, "The Louisiana study may show that patterns of heart disease formed in childhood by diet, behavior and other factors become self sustaining in adults even when the childhood causes seem to disappear."[7]

Of particular interest in relation to Type A behavior in children is some recent research relating the child-rearing practices of Type A and Type B mothers with their Type A and Type B sons. Psychologist Karen Matthews of the University of Pittsburg writes:

> *The results revealed that Type A boys were treated differently from Type B boys. Specifically, Type A and Type B mothers gave fewer positive evaluations of task performance to Type A boys than to Type B boys, and Type A boys were pushed harder than were Type B boys, particularly by Type B mothers. An example of the latter is, "you're doing fine, but next time let's try for 5" (a higher score on the test the boy had taken).*[8]

It is not always clear just what is cause and what is effect in such studies but the indicators are that parental hurrying can be related to Type A behavior in children.

Perhaps the most serious implication of this research is that patterns of reaction to stress established in childhood can be carried over into adulthood and become autonomous. Hurried children, for example, may not show serious symptoms in childhood but may carry with them patterns of emotional response that can lead to serious illness as adults. The child who gets tension headaches will, in all likelihood, be the adult who experiences migraine headaches. Excessive stress in childhood can have life-long effects by producing patterns of stress reaction that stay with the young person throughout life.

SCHOOL BURNOUT

When a person's job places him or her in a situation of chronic unrelieved stress, the end result is what has come to be called "job burnout." Usually what happens is that the person loses all enthusiasm for the job, hates to go to work, and is either lethargic and constantly tired or always tense with nervous energy. Physical symptoms like tension headaches and high blood pressure or behavioral symptoms like drug and alcohol abuse are common. The end result is that the person either quits or gets fired from the job.

Going to school is the job or occupation of children and adolescents. As we have seen, schools are academically oriented; children have to learn the tool skills and basic knowledge about science, social studies, and literature. But not all young people are academically oriented, and even those who are may not learn best under the competitive, test-regulated school program. For young people who may be interested in farming, animal husbandry, forestry, carpentry, plumbing, automotive mechanics, and so on, the academic thrust of schools, particularly high schools, is frustrating. And it is also frustrating for students who cannot keep up with the unrelenting academic pressure.

For such young people, school is like a bad job. It imposes chronic stress on them, and the symptoms of school burnout begin to appear. Often these young people hate to go to school and stay home because of sickness whenever they can. They are frequently tardy and often cut class. Many begin to use and abuse alcohol and drugs; occasionally they vandalize the school or deface it with crude graffiti. Eventually, they drop out of school as soon as it is legally possible. In the high-pressure school systems of the Northeast, school dropouts are on the rise again after more than a decade of stability.

Students who burn out at school rarely go back to complete their high school diploma. One study of high school dropouts showed that about 75 percent of the males had had some form of military training and the rest held either nonskilled jobs or had received training on the job. Of the young women who had dropped out, 40 percent became housewives, 30 percent were employed in nonskilled jobs, and 30 percent were secretaries or clerks.

In their study of job burnout Robert L. Veninga and James P. Spradley identified what they said were five stages in job burnout: 1) the honeymoon, 2) fuel shortage, 3) chronic symptoms, 4) crises, and 5) hitting the wall.[9] Roughly the same stages seem to occur with young people who have undergone school burnout. A child begins school eagerly and happily with high expectations (the honeymoon). But soon the endless demands for learning in a nonsupportive environment and the competition force the young person to call upon energy reserves that are not always replenished. The result (fuel shortage) is exemplified in the child's dissatisfaction with school, fatigue, poor work habits, and sleep disturbances.

When children have to drag themselves to school day after day to face repeated failure, they sometimes develop chronic symptoms, which can be physical or psychological. Allergies, for example, are exacerbated by chronic, unrelieved stress. Proneness to accident and illness can be byproducts of unrelieved school stress. Headaches, ulcers, and colitis can also be symptoms. Some children show behavioral symptoms like aggressive bullying or quiet withdrawal. Still others become "Alibi Ikes" who invent elaborate excuses and justifications for their repeated school failures.

Excessive drug and alcohol use are also symptoms of school burnout. Consider the following account which appeared recently in the Hartford *Courant*:

> *The four students crouching behind a car in a visitors' parking lot of Hall High School in West Hartford were getting ready to take a test.*
>
> *But no textbooks were open and none of the students was studying notes, they were passing around a marijuana cigarette.*
>
> *"We're mellowing out," said one student.*
>
> *"Relaxing so we can do well on the test," said another. "We have to get a good grade."*[10]

Another symptom of incipient school burnout is chronic cheating. Again an account from the Hartford *Courant*:

> *At Westport's Staples High School five young men were taking a calculus quiz. They squirmed in their chairs as their teacher walked around the room surveying the students' progress. The five students' heads bobbed up and down as they glanced from the test to the teacher waiting for him to turn his back. He did and they cheated by exchanging papers. They, too, had to get good grades.*[11]

In the first stages of school burnout, the initial challenge and excitement are replaced by dissatisfaction and unhappiness which are dealt with in a variety of symptoms, or stress valves. If these stress valves don't work, or if they come to be overused, a *crisis* can result. What happens then is that the symptoms become so severe that the young person has to remain home from school or manages to get himself or herself expelled from school. The stresses of school have become unbearable and the safety valves used before no longer work.

Consider the case of Timothy K (not his real name):

> *Timothy looked forward to going to school because his older brothers and sisters talked about all the interesting things they did there and teased him because he did not know the alphabet and couldn't count. So Timothy began kindergarten eager to learn. But somehow he couldn't quite get the hang of those marks on the paper. He would confuse b's and d's and would read "saw" as "was." Sometimes the other children laughed and the teacher did not say anything to them. Timothy felt as if she was laughing at him too.*
>
> *School wasn't as much fun as Timothy thought it was going to be. It wasn't fun at all. Timothy began being tired and it was hard for his mother to get him up in the morning. He became draggy and had to be hurried through his washing, dressing and eating. If his mother was not after him every minute he would stop what he was doing and seem to be lost in a trance or a daydream. Often his mother had to drive him to school because he was so late. Then he was reluctant to get out of the car and seemed to have to drag himself up the walk to the school steps. This pattern continued as Timothy showed the signs of fuel shortage and chronic symptoms.*
>
> *Then one day Timothy's mother was called to come to the school immediately. She went to the principal's office where a defiant Timothy sat rigidly in his chair, black eyes ablaze, fingers clenched, lower lip clenched tightly by his upper teeth. "We have a problem," the principal said. "Timothy was openly rude to his teacher, he not only talked back, he swore at her and now he refuses to apologize," His mother was distraught and insisted that Timothy apologize that minute to his teacher who was standing*

*there. But Timothy remained mute, his eyes still spitting
defiance. The principal told his mother to take Timothy
home and not to bring him back until he was ready to tell
his teacher he was sorry and to behave like a responsible
student.*

Timothy had reached the crisis stage of school burnout; his
symptoms had become critical. It was at this point that Timothy was
brought to see me. What I had to do, first of all, was to defuse the
crisis atmosphere. Timothy's mother was sure the world had come
to an end and Timothy would have been glad if it had. I talked a little
about the fact that Timothy was far from unique, that many other
children had hard times at school, said something nasty, and
refused to retract it. Timothy and his mother needed to know that he
was not off the continuum of the human race. What Timothy needed
was to feel good about himself again and to get a sense that he could
succeed at school. He needed to be able to forgive himself before he
was able to forgive his teacher and say he was sorry.

The fifth stage of school burnout is less common than the others
because most children are taken out of the situation before "hitting
the wall" occurs. The phrase "hitting the wall" is taken from the
experience in long distance running when the runner feels that
every last ounce of reserve has been exhausted and that he or she
cannot run another step. The experience is like trying to run against
a cement wall. Physically, all the blood sugar (glycogen) stored in the
muscles is used up, the body becomes dehydrated, and there is a loss
of blood volume. The person experiences dizziness, fainting, muscle
paralysis, and sometimes complete collapse.

Although "hitting the wall" is infrequent, one still sees it in the
high school student who has studied so hard for college entrance
exams that he or she is too physically spent to take the exams. Often
the response is not to the particular set of exams but rather to the
accumulated stress of a long history of exam taking which has taken
its toll of the young person's reserve energy.

Not all young people who go to school and compete for grades,
scholarships, and so on experience school burnout. Many young people seem to thrive on the stress of school and academic pressure. It
is not just the stress of schooling but how the stress is perceived and
responded to that will determine whether or not the young person
experiences school burnout.

LEARNED HELPLESSNESS

One stress reaction in children that has been extensively studied is "learned helplessness." In general, helplessness is what we experience when events around us are beyond our control. I recall, for example, when I was a young man going into the hospital for minor surgery—the removal of a benign cyst. As I was being rolled into the operating room and as the anesthesia began to take effect, I heard the nurse say, "It's all right, young man, your appendix will be out in no time." I remember trying to protest but was unable to speak or move. Before going out completely I experienced a profound sense of helplessness and lack of control as to what was being done to me. Fortunately it was the cyst and not my appendix that was removed.

In the situation described above, I felt helpless because (a) something bad was about to happen to me and (b) there was nothing I could do to avoid it even though I knew it was coming. Helplessness always involves the sense of impending danger to oneself or one's loved ones and also the awareness that there is nothing one can do personally to help the situation. Every parent who has ever taken his or her child to an emergency room, and seen the child whisked away by strangers in white, knows the stress of helplessness, the knowledge of danger, the inability or impossibility of taking appropriate action. Helplessness is a kind of second-order stress; it is the stress of not being able to respond to stress.

We now know, thanks to the work of Martin Seligman and his students and associates, that the helplessness response, the feeling that we cannot help ourselves or others, can be learned.[12] Children, for example, can learn to feel helpless, to feel threatened and unable to take action, even when this is not the case. Such children become withdrawn, listless, and apathetic and seem to lose all motivation for learning and for relating to other children.

Much research has now been done to show that when some people experience situations over which they have no control, they tend to give up and not perform well. In one study, for example, college students were exposed to escapable, nonescapable, or no loud noise. Afterwards they were asked to solve anagram problems like IATOP (PATIO). Students who had been exposed to inescapable noise were much less successful than students who were exposed to escapable noise or no noise. Apparently, students who have been put in a helpless position carry that attitude over to other situations.

Consider the following case reported by Seligman:

> *In the early hours of a February morning in 1971, a powerful earthquake struck Los Angeles. Marshall's experience was typical for an eight year old in the San Fernando Valley, the epicenter of the quake: He awakened at 5:45 to find himself in what sounded like a railroad tunnel, with a train bearing down upon him. The floor undulated; he screamed and from the next room heard the frightened screams of his mother and father. Although it was only thirty seconds, it seemed like an eternity of terror while the very ground shook beneath him.*
>
> > *Three years later, Marshall still showed psychological aftereffects of that morning. He was timid and jumpy; slight unexpected sounds terrified him. He had trouble getting to sleep, and once he had, his sleep was very light and restless; he occasionally woke up screaming.*[13]

Many children acquire learned helplessness at school when they are confronted with learning tasks that are too difficult for their level of ability. Some children, for example, fail to learn to read because the way in which it is taught confronts them with a task they cannot comprehend or control. Under these circumstances the learned helplessness response is produced and the child retreats from any experience having to do with reading:

> *Victor was a slow starter when reading instruction began in kindergarten and first grade. He was eager, but just wasn't ready to make the connection between words on paper and speech. He tried hard at first, but made no progress; his answers, readily volunteered, were consistently wrong. The more he failed, the more reluctant to try he became; he said less and less in class. By second grade, although he participated eagerly in music and art, when reading came around he became sullen. His teacher gave him special drilling for awhile but they both soon gave up. By this time he might have been ready to read, but simply seeing a word card or a spelling book would set off a tan-*

trum of sullenness or of defiant aggression. This attitude
began to spread to the rest of his school day. He vacillated
between being dependent and being a hellion.[14]

In a sense, the learned helplessness described by Seligman is
the obverse of the Type A personality described earlier. Both are
exaggerations of the fight or flight reaction, and both are rigid and
inflexibile. Faced with an important situation over which he or she
has no control, the Type A child goes all out while the learned helplessness child totally retreats and gives up. In neither case is there a
realistic assessment of the situation or a consideration of alternatives. As a result of the stress of hurrying, children may be condi-
tioned to patterns of response that are rigid and inflexible and that
stay with them and become their adult patterns of reaction to stress.

PREMATURE STRUCTURING

Freud was once asked what became of the clever shoe-shine boys so
common on the streets of Vienna around the turn of the century.
These boys, street wise and witty, were able to charm their cus-
tomers into giving them big tips. Freud reflected a moment and then
replied, "They become cobblers." In a sense these children had
grown up too fast and as a consequence were not able to go further.
Their characters had become structured so early there was little
room for further growth and differentiation of personality.

Premature structuring is most often seen in children who have
trained from an early age in one or another sport or performing art.
What often happens is that the child becomes so specialized so early
that other parts of his or her personality are somewhat undevel-
oped. Some tennis stars, who have been trained since childhood to
be champions, can talk about little else than tennis off the courts.
Other adults who were overspecialized as children show rather
strange behavior as adults: Bobby Fisher, the chess master, is a
recluse and is socially quite inept.

Hurrying children into a sport or a performing art need not
result in premature structuring and personality constriction.
Yehudi Menuhin, who played difficult concerts with leading symphony orchestras at the age of seven, is an example. He was blessed

not only with talent but also with parents who put his career and needs before their own but without the exploitative motive of realizing themselves through their son. He was also blessed with gifted and extraordinarily devoted teachers. These teachers were major performing artists of the period who would even stop by his house to tune his violin for him.

But many other child prodigies are not that lucky. The child prodigy is as likely to fade as to become a superstar. "One such example in recent years is Lilit Gampel. At age twelve Lilit's nationally televised performance of Mendelssohn's concerto with the Boston Pops won her a contract with Columbia Artists Management and a score of engagements with symphony orchestras in Europe and the United States. But for the California wunderkind, all the travelling, including regular visits to a new teacher in New York, the late Ivan Galamian, proved too much. Her playing slipped, she could manage fewer and fewer concerts, relations with her too ambitious parents grew strained and even early admission to Juliard on a full scholarship failed to pull her out of the slump. Colleagues from her performing days say that except for a stint with a small New Jersey orchestra Lilit simply dropped out of sight."[15]

An even more tragic case is that of Chrisian Kriens. "A celebrated Dutch prodigy, Kriens excelled at conducting and composing as well as at the violin and piano, but he ended up as a disc jockey in Hartford, where in his early twenties, he committed suicide."[16]

Some of the stresses encountered by children who achieve early include conflicts between school and practice time and the incessant interviews with the media. According to Howard Gardner of Harvard, every prodigy goes through what he calls the "midlife crisis of the prodigy." As children, prodigies perform out of curiosity, out of the challenge of learning and for the approval of parents. But when they become adolescents, they begin to raise questions like: "Why am I doing this, who am I doing it for? Some may decide they just don't want the pressure and that is their right. Others will decide to continue, but in their own way."[17]

Premature structuring has always been true of low-income families, who were more likely than middle-class families to be single-parent homes, to have both parents working, and not to be school oriented. Children in low-income homes work early, attain independence early, marry and have families early. But it makes sense to low-income young people because they can see the need for their independence, working, and so on.

But now middle-income parents are often single parents, and many middle-income families have both parents working. So middle-income children are now being hurried to grow up fast, are being prematurely structured, for the same reasons low-income children are, namely, parental need. But the parental needs of middle-income parents are different from those of low-income parents; they don't need children to do chores or earn money. The middle-income child is supported materially but hurried socially and intellectually to serve parental ego need, not parental material need.

Like the prodigy, the hurried child takes stock in adolescence and asks, "What am I doing" and "Why am I doing it?" If the answer is that it is for parents and not for the self, the young person may revolt in any number of different ways such as by running away, getting into drugs, dropping out of school, becoming delinquent, or simply refusing to perform. In every case young people are giving evidence that premature structuring, growing up fast to satisfy parental ego needs without concern for their own needs, is not acceptable.

THE INVULNERABLES

When I worked for the family court in Denver, Colorado, and later in Rochester, New York, I dealt primarily with delinquent children. Occasionally I was able to see the whole family and that was sometimes a surprise. For example, I once saw a fourteen-year-old girl who, with a friend, had been "tricking it" in a trailer parked near an air force base. The mother was obese, on welfare, and was frequented by many men. The father was long since gone. But the younger sister, ten years old, was doing fine; she was a straight A student and was well liked by her teachers and peers.

Such children have often been ignored in psychological and psychiatric research which has focused upon pathology rather than health. As Lois Murphy wrote in 1962: "It is something of a paradox that a nation which has exulted in its rapid expansion and its scientific, technological achievements should have developed in its studies of childhood so vast a problem literature. . . . The language of problems, difficulties, inadequacies, of antisocial or delinquent conduct, or of ambivalence and anxiety, is familiar. We know there are devices for correcting, bypassing, or overcoming threats, but for the most part these have not been directly studied."[18] In effect, the helping professions too have hurried children into categories of pathology and disturbance that were once reserved for adults.

But in the last decade there has been increasing interest in those young people who respond positively to stress. Foremost in this work is psychiatrist E. J. Anthony of St. Louis University and psychologist Norman Garmezy of the University of Minnesota. Both were at first interested in "children at risk"—children of schizophrenic parents who were more likely than the offspring of nonschizophrenic parents to develop symptoms of mental illness. Both investigators noticed that some young people who, by all that is sacred in clinical psychiatry and psychology, should be ill, were not. They then began to study these children to glean some understanding of effective ways of coping with overwhelming stress.

The following case described by Dr. Garmezy provides an example: "In the slums of Minneapolis, there is a 10-year-old boy who lives in a dilapidated apartment with his father, an ex-convict now dying of cancer, his illiterate mother, and seven brothers and sisters, two of whom are mentally retarded. Yet, his teachers describe him as an unusually competent child who does well in his studies and is loved by almost everyone in his school."[19]

And Dr. Anthony reports on the different reactions of three children whose schizophrenic mother believed that someone was poisoning the food at home. The oldest girl, a twelve-year-old, shared her mother's fears and refused to eat except in a restaurant. The middle child, who was about ten years old, also refused to eat at home—except when her father was there. But the seven-year-old son ate at home every day. When Anthony asked him how he could do so, the boy shrugged and said, "Well I'm not dead yet." He was an invulnerable. Yet his older sister eventually became as psychotic as her mother. The middle child remained sane and did moderately well, although she had occasional symptoms of maladjustment. The boy, however, went on to a brilliant career. "His mother's illness gave him a tremendous need to overcome obstacles, to cope with problems," says Anthony. "He seemed to see the environment as a sort of challenge."

What enables these young people to cope so well with stress? Researchers suggest that at least five different qualities are involved:

1. *Social competence.* Invulnerables seem at ease with peers and adults and make others at ease with them. It is almost as if they have taken a Dale Carnegie course in "How to Make Friends and Influence People."

2. *Impression management.* Invulnerables are able to present themselves as appealing and charming. They seem to really like adults, not in a dependent way but rather in a way that suggests that they have much to learn and are willing to do so. It is a subservience with pride that is most attractive and wins adults over to them as mentors.

3. *Self-confidence.* Such children have a sense of their own competence and ability to master stress situations. Accordingly, they see problems as a challenge rather than as evidence of their incompetence. Garmezy tells of one child who made "bread sandwiches" so that she would give the appearance of having a lunch like her friends even if there was no filling. "Bread sandwiches" became a metaphor for her whenever she had to cope with a difficult problem. "I guess I will just have to make a bread sandwich."

4. *Independence.* Invulnerables are independent and are not swayed by suggestion. In effect, they think for themselves and are not dissuaded by persons in authority or power. They often find a place for themselves where they can find privacy, peace, and a chance to create an environment suitable to their needs and interests.

5. *Achievement.* Invulnerables are producers. They get good grades, have hobbies, write poetry, sculpt, paint, do carpentry, and so on. Many are exceptionally original and creative. Many develop intense interests at an early age. Perhaps, had they been born to a different family, they would have been prodigies. But born into stressful home situations, some of their strengths and talents seem to be directed to the most important task—survival.

We are just beginning to learn what factors lead some children to become case hardened in the crucible of stress. Some of what we know can be used in suggesting ways of combating stress in all children. But it is also true that invulnerables may be gifted children who in other circumstances would have outstanding careers. Such children are a good example of nature-nurture interaction. In a favorable environment a bright, creative child is gifted; in an unfavorable, stressful environment he or she is an invulnerable.

These are but some of the ways in which children react to the stress of hurrying. Emotional distress and behavioral disturbance can no longer be traced to conflict alone. Today, disturbed children have to be seen, evaluated, and helped within the context of an overwhelmingly stressful environment. If anything, the children we see in the clinic today are more like the shell shock victims (the war neuroses) of battle than the neurotic children of the past. In a sense, war is to adults what hurrying is to children—an enormous stress which brings much harm and some good.

Chapter 9

Helping Hurried Children

O urs is a hurried and hurrying society. We are always on the lookout for ways of doing things faster and more expeditiously. We have the supermarket to speed up shopping and fast-food restaurants to speed up eating. We build super highways to speed up transportation and household gadgets to speed up housework. And the current revolution in information processing will dramatically speed up the work done in offices. We even hurry our recreation with automated pinsetters, golf carts, and ball tossers. And designers work hard to increase speed for leisure craft, whether driven by motor or sail. We are a time-oriented and time-regulated society, and we impart these values to our children. What is the first expensive utilitarian gift we usually give our children? A watch. We hurry our children because we hurry ourselves.

Although the pressure to get things done more quickly and efficiently has positive benefits—it has made us the most innovative society on earth—it has its drawbacks, such as producing impatience. For all our technological finesse and sophisticated facade, we are a people who cannot—will not—wait. Compulsive about punctuality and using our time most efficiently, we become surly when forced to relax and wait our turn. We switch lines in a bank or grocery store if we think another cashier is faster; we leave waiters less of a tip if service is slow; and when traveling we are willing to pay a high premium to arrive at our destination as quickly as possible—whether we are going abroad, to another city, or to visit friends across town. Only in the context of a society that is hell-bent on doing jobs more quickly and better and is impatient with waiting and inefficiency can we really understand the phenomenon of hurried children and hope to help them.

What can we do to help children who are being pressured to grow up fast and who experience this as inordinate stress? First of all, it is important to recognize what we cannot do. We cannot change the basic thrust of American society for which hurrying is the accepted and valued way of life. Nor can we eliminate the abiding impatience that goes along with hurrying. When hurrying reflects cultural values like being punctual, then urging children to be on time has social justification. But the *abuse of hurrying* harms children. When hurrying serves parental or institutional needs at the expense of children without imbuing them with redeeming social values, the result on the child is negative.

The abuse of hurrying is a contractual violation. Contractual violations are experienced as exploitative and stressful by children because the implicit contracts between parents and children are the fundament of the children's sense of basic trust, a kind of standard against which the children's social interactions are measured. If something happens to a child's sense of basic trust, the sense that the world is a safe and benevolent place and the sense that people are well meaning and caring are damaged, so to is the child's sense of self and his or her trust in interpersonal relations.

Two different types of contractual violation and exploitation can be identified. One is qualitative and might be called *developmental hurrying*. It occurs whenever we ask children to understand beyond their limits of understanding, to decide beyond their capacity to make decisions, or to act wilfully before they have the will to act. But children can also be hurried quantitatively, and this might be called *energic hurrying*. We engage in energic hurrying whenever, through our hurrying, we force children to call upon their energy reserves.

All of us have engaged in developmental or energic hurrying at times. Firstborn children, for example, are often subject to developmental hurrying because new parents are unfamiliar with children; thus, not surprisingly, many firstborns are hurried children—hard working, competitive, driving. Likewise, we all engage in energic hurrying when we take young children on long trips. Children can accommodate to such contractual violations because they are not experienced as evidence of rejection or lack of caring.

However, when developmental or energic hurrying occurs because the parent or parents habitually place their own needs ahead of the child's, hurrying can produce real damage. Contracting is based upon mutuality, with the needs of parent and child in more or less rough balance. When parental need routinely takes precedent over child need, developmental and energic hurrying is perceived as stressful to children, even though sometimes putting our needs ahead of children's is inadvertent rather than deliberate. One way we can help keep track of whether or not we are unreasonably hurrying our children is to periodically review our contractual relationships by making some lists, like the one below of our current contractual arrangements.

Contract Evaluation Form

Child
Age
Sex

Contract 1

Achievements expected   Supports provided

Contract 2

Responsibilities expected   Freedoms provided

Contract 3

Loyalities expected   Commitments provided

In filling out these forms there should be a reasonable balance between achievements and supports, responsibilities and freedoms, and loyalties and commitments. If it is easy to specify what you expect in terms of achievement, responsibility, and loyalty but difficult to itemize what you provide in the way of support, freedom, and commitment, you may be committing some contractual violations and may want to add to your side of the contractual arrangement.

With respect to developmental hurrying, it is useful to compare your list of expectations with the kinds of capacities children have (as outlined in Chapter Five). If the expectations are unreasonable for children at that stage, some developmental hurrying may be going on, and you may want to revise your expectations. Looking at the balance sheet, you can decide whether or not there is any abuse of hurrying.

THE CHILD'S PERCEPTION OF HURRYING

If we are asking too much and hurrying our children developmentally or energically, we can either cut back on our demands or increase our supports. This is an objective way of helping children deal with hurrying in the sense that it deals with the actual, often unverbalized expectancies that we have of our children and with the amount and variety of supports we are willing to offer.

But hurrying, like any stressor, has a subjective dimension. How children perceive hurrying determines its effects as much as the fact of hurrying itself. We know, for example, that children of about eight years and younger tend to engage in "magical thinking"—they often believe that their wishes, feelings, or acts bear a causal relationship to parental acts. To illustrate, many young people feel that something they did (teased daddy about his beard) or felt (anger at daddy for not buying a toy gun) caused daddy to go away. They may also deprive themselves of some treat (not eat candy) or sacrifice a favored toy (by giving it away or breaking it) in hopes that these magical acts will bring daddy back.

How children perceive hurrying, then, will depend in part on their level of mental development; it will also depend on their temperament, past experience, intelligence, and so on. We as parents or teachers need to look a little more closely at how children in the four major stages of development view hurrying and what we can do to make those perceptions less stressful. It is important, however, to step back from our adult perspective and recognize that there is more than one way to perceive reality.

Young children (two to eight years) tend to perceive hurrying as a rejection, as evidence that their parents do not really care about them. Children are very emotionally astute in this regard and tune in to what is a partial truth. To a certain extent, hurrying children

from one caretaker to another each day, or into academic achievement, or into making decisions they are not really able to make *is* a
rejection. It is a rejection of the children as they see themselves, of
what they are capable of coping with and doing. Children find such
rejection very threatening and often develop stress symptoms as a
result.

Children at this stage take the part for the whole. They sense a
little rejection in the parent and take it for the whole of the parental
attitude. Young children are not relativistic but, rather, think in absolute terms. (Literature for young children is replete with one-
dimensional characters such as witches, ogres, fairy godmothers,
and prince charmings.) So, when we engage in some necessary
hurrying, our young children may misperceive a part of our attitude
for the whole and miss our very real love and concern for them in
their global and undifferentiated perception of a bit of rejection.

The situation with young children is compounded by what I
have found to be an almost universal assumption on the part of
adults regarding young children: we tend to assume that children
are much more like us in their thoughts than they are in their feelings. But in fact, just the reverse is true: *children are most like us in
their feelings and least like us in their thoughts.* Below is an example
of the response of a two-year-old to his father's devastating cerebral
hemorrhage, which left the man retarded and helpless. The outburst
occurred when the mother and son went for counseling. The mother
reports:

> *Will stopped playing and stared. Then all at once, he*
> *started picking up toys and throwing them around the*
> *room viciously, as hard as he could. I thought "Oh God,*
> *what am I doing here?" I had had a perfectly happy little*
> *boy. Then my little Will ran over and started hitting me. I*
> *was mortified. I was furious at the counselor, but before I*
> *could speak, she had calmly knelt next to Will and was*
> *quietly explaining that it was okay to throw toys because*
> *they were only toys; and while he certainly didn't have a*
> *right to hit his mother, he certainly had a right to be mad at*
> *her.*
>
> *"Mom didn't take care of everything, did she, Will?"*
> *the counselor asked.*

187

> *"No," said Will with feeling, "she didn't. She let my*
> *daddy get sick and I hate her." Carefully and at length the*
> *counselor explained that even doctors had no way to keep*
> *Daddy from getting sick and neither did Mommy . . . then*
> *Will climbed into his mother's lap, clung to her and*
> *sobbed. "I was astonished," Will's mother concluded, "I*
> *never dreamed that two-year-olds have such deep feel-*
> *ings."[1]*

Accordingly, when we have to hurry young children, when they have to be at a day-care center or with a baby-sitter, we need to appreciate children's feelings about the matter. Giving children a rational explanation, "I have to work so we can eat, buy clothes, and so on," helps but it isn't enough to deal with the child's implicit thought—"If they really love me, they wouldn't go off and leave me." We need to respond to a child's feeling more than to his or her intellect. One might say, for instance: "I'm really going to miss you today and wish you could be with me." The exact words are less important than the message that the separation is painful but necessary for you too. And it is equally important, when you pick your child up at the end of the day, to say something about how happy you are to see him or her. By responding to the young child's feelings, we lessen some of the stress of hurrying.

Sometimes our tendency to think of children as not sharing our feelings leads us to compound the stress of hurrying in a different way. When we are in a hurry we are sometimes impolite and thoughtless to young children because we assume they are not as concerned about such things as we are. But children are very sensitive to signs of parental caring. If we need to break a promise about taking a child to a movie, the park, or the zoo, it is very important that we apologize and make it clear that we really are sorry. In the same way, when we ask children to do something for us, to save us time, or to help us out, it is really important to say "please" and "thank you." Being polite to children speaks to their feelings of self-worth (as it does to adults), which are always threatened when we hurry them. Being polite to children helps them to perceive hurrying in a less stressful way.

Being polite to children is very important and may do as much for improving parent-child relations as many of the more elaborate parental strategies that are currently being proposed. The essence of good manners is not the ability to say the right words at the right time but, rather, thoughtfulness and consideration of others. When we are polite to children we show in the most simple and direct way possible that we value them as people and care about their feelings. Thus politeness is one of the most simple and effective ways of easing stress in children and of helping them to become thoughtful and sensitive people themselves.

Once children attain school age and the concrete operations described by Piaget (see Chapter Five), they begin to view hurrying in more complex ways. At the deepest emotional level, they still experience hurrying as a kind of rejection. But instead of blaming themselves or their parents, they use their new mental abilities to rationalize parental behavior and to find acceptable, rather than real, reasons for hurrying. This is why, for example, prodigies do not question parental hurrying during childhood. At this stage, children either accept the rationale offered by their parents or construct their own.

School-age children are more independent and more self-reliant than young children. Consequently, they often seem to welcome hurrying in the sense that they are eager to take on adult chores and responsibilities, particularly in single-parent homes, where they may try intuitively to fill the role of the absent parent. The danger with this age group is for parents to accept this display of maturity for true maturity rather than for what it is—a kind of game. The image to keep in mind for this age group is Peter Pan, who wanted to assume some adult responsibilities (leadership, protection, etc.) but did not really want to grow up and take on some of the negative qualities that children perceive as characteristic of adults. Children want to play at being grown up but they really don't want adults to take them too seriously.

For this age group, it is important that we communicate our appreciation for all that they do for us—helping around the house, baby sitting and so on—but also that we know they are still children and that there are some things they should not be burdened with. To illustrate, when the oldest child feels that he or she is old enough to baby sit the younger ones but we do not, it is important to say that we feel good about their wanting to help and that we will be happy to let them baby sit when the young ones are a little bigger and easier to manage. By setting limits and by suggesting that the limits are as much a function of the younger children's immaturity as of their own, we can communicate our awareness of their willingness to be grown up but also of their desire to retain the prerogatives of children.

As young people move into adolescence and attain new, more complex mental abilities, hurrying is again seen in a new way. Although adolescents also perceive hurrying as a rejection at a deep young-child level, they begin to see it in more abstract, complex terms. First of all, adolescents construct concepts of ideal parents who are all-knowing, all-good, and all-generous and then compare their real parents with this ideal and find them sadly wanting. This is one reason why young adolescents criticize their parents for the way they dress, eat, talk, look, act, and so on. And when adolescents feel hurried by parents the criticism often reaches a frenzy. If we summarize the way in which the three age groups react to hurrying, we might say that young children tend to blame themselves, children tend to blame the world, and adolescents tend to blame their parents.

Secondly, adolescents not only blame their parents for hurrying them as adolescents but also for hurrying them as children. While school-age children rationalize parental hurrying, they don't forget it. In effect, *adolescents pay us back in the teen years for all the sins, real or imagined, that we committed against them when they were children.* As parents, we really need to begin preparing for our children's adolescence when they are in the cradle. By the time they are fully grown it is often too late to be thoughtful of their feelings.

Dealing with adolescents is complicated, to say the least. Their newfound intellectual abilities make them formidable opponents in any argument, and their size, strength, and physical maturity wipe out any previous physical inequalities. What needs to be kept in mind is that adolescents still care about their parents and want to be cared about. Now they resist hurrying directly because they feel that it is a violation of parental contracting, that it is a kind of exploitation. But it is because they want to be cared about that they react so strongly to contractual violations. Perhaps they really do not want to admit how much they care and want to be cared about. Accordingly, contractual violations are painful, at least in part because such violations force the adolescent to ackowledge how much she or he is still dependent upon parental love. In any case, in my experience with delinquent young people, the most common feeling expressed was one of exploitation, of being used by parents who put their own needs ahead of their children's.

Adolescents, then, in contrast to children, clearly perceive hurrying as a breach of contract and as exploitation by parents. In dealing with this perception of hurrying, we must recognize that this is the young person's reality. Although parents may have perfectly good reasons for doing what they are doing, young people do not see it in the same way. And arguing with an adolescent usually has just the opposite of the intended effect. When adolescents say that they should not have the responsibility of cleaning up their rooms, doing the dishes, or caring for younger siblings, there is little point to arguing the issue. Adolescents see such demands as their being pushed into responsibilities that are, to their way of thinking, not really theirs but someone else's. They are exempt, by virtue of being adolescents, from doing mundane chores. Arguing with adolescents merely entrenches them in their position.

What is a parent to do? Well, as the old saying goes, "If you can't beat them, join them." Sometimes it helps to accept the young person's premise or perception of the situation and to proceed from there. In working with delinquents, for example, I used to argue with them about their negative perceptions of their parents. They would tell me how bad their parents were and I would try and point out the efforts the parents had made to help the situation, but to no avail. The more I defended the parents, the more the adolescents attacked them. Then I decided to try another approach. I started to agree with them. "Yes, you are right, I see what you mean, they really are an awful set of parents. Poor thing, you, really got stuck with a couple of bummers." At which point the young delinquent almost invariably said, "Hey, c'mon Doc, they are really not that bad!"

So one strategy in dealing with adolescents' perception of hurrying as exploitation is to accept their perception as correct at least for them. The middle ground between totally accepting their reality and totally rejecting it is the acceptance of the fact that while we can recognize that their reality is valid for them, it is not necessarily valid for us. We might say, "Okay, I know that you feel what I am asking you to do is unreasonable. I don't think so, but I can appreciate that you might see it that way. What do you think are reasonable responsibilities for a person your age in our circumstances?" Often, when this question is asked, young people list a set of responsibilities much more stringent than the ones the parents have laid down. Unfortunately, this is usually not enough to get young people to do what we ask. It does, however, help them perceive our position more realistically and to acknowledge that it is laziness, procrastination, or some other reason, rather than parental exploitation that is at issue. This diffuses the emotional impact and lessens the stress, which is probably as much as can be hoped for.

Thus children perceive hurrying differently than we do. If we want to reduce some of the stress of the inevitable hurrying that all children in our society experience, it is important to appreciate the particular way in which they perceive the hurrying. To do this, we have to decenter from our own adult perspective. Since we are committed to our realities as much as children are to theirs, this is not always an easy thing to do. It is even more difficult when we are under stress; when we are stressed we become egocentric and have trouble seeing the world from another person's perspective.

In these transitional and stressful times, it is particularly important that we try and look at the world the way in which hurried children do. Only when we start from their view of the world can we really hope to help them acknowledge our reality that hurrying is not rejection and that contractual violation is really not exploitation.

PLAY: AN ANTIDOTE TO HURRYING

So far we have talked mainly about what parents might do to help hurried children, but as we have seen, schools and media hurry children too. While it is not always possible to change schools and media, concerted efforts have been effective. Parent groups, for example, have encouraged a number of school systems to offer alternative educational programs so that parents can choose between, say, a curriculum-centered or a child-centered program. Likewise, Action for Children's Television (ACT) has been very effective in getting programers to cut down on violence, on advertisements for sugared foods, and so on. Parent groups can succeed in getting schools and media to de-center and to take the children's point of view. This is particularly important in the domain of children's play.

Unfortunately, both the value and the meaning of play are poorly understood in our hurried society. Indeed, what happened to adults in our society has now happened to children—play has been transformed into work. What was once recreational—sports, summer camp, musical training—is now professionalized and competitive. In schools, when budgets are tight, the first subjects to be cut are art, music, and drama. And the media, suffused with the new realism, offer little in the way of truly imaginative fantasy. Perhaps the best evidence of the extent to which our children are hurried is the lack of opportunities for genuine play available to them.

What is play and why is it so important to growing children? Over the years, there have been many theories of play, each of which has contained some aspect of truth. Philosopher Herbert Spencer regarded play as a means of reducing "surplus energy."[2] According to Spencer, we have more energy than we need to adapt to modern society, and the surplus is "burned off" in play that has no productive purpose. Around the turn of the century, biologist Karl Groos wrote a two-volume work on the play of animals and humans in which he argued that play was a "preparation for life."[3] He noted that young animals play at stalking games (such as a young kitten playing with a ball of twine, or a cat playing with a mouse) which as adults they use in catching prey. In a like manner, when children play house, they are engaging in preparatory activity for assuming adult roles. Groos also pointed out, however, that play was a preparation for aesthetic appreciation.

Groos's theory that play was a preparation for life was very influential in educational circles. Italian educator Maria Montessori made it a tenet of her educational program. Her approach to education, which is currently enjoying enormous interest in this country, transformed Groos's theory into a simple formula that has become a kind of motto for contemporary early childhood education: "play is the child's work." Montessori, who worked first with retarded and then with slum children in Italy, had little use for play or fantasy as ends in themselves. She wrote:

> *Imagination has always been given a predominant place in the psychology of childhood and all over the world, people tell their children fairy stories which are enjoyed immensely, as if children wanted to exercise this great gift, as*

imagination undoubtedly is. Yet when all are agreed that a child loves to imagine, why do we give him only fairy tales and toys on which to practice this gift? If a child can imagine a fairy and a fairyland, it will not be difficult for him to imagine America. Instead of hearing it vaguely in conversation, he can help to clarify his own ideas of it by looking at the globe on which it is shown.[4]

This attitude toward play as subordinate to social adaptation and as preparation for life had a brief vogue in this country, as did Montessori education just before the First World War. But Montessori's ideas came under attack by American educators at the time when Freud's work was becoming better known and went into decline between the two world wars as the Freudian influence on education was waxing strong. For Freud, play was important in its own right as a kind of safety valve for dealing with societal repressions. Dreams, jokes, and drama were all forms of play in the broad sense. They were all socially acceptable ways of discharging socially unacceptable feelings, wishes, and desires. This view of play became distorted in some variants of progressive education. In such schools it was felt that any control of the child's impulses would lead to repression and neurosis. The attitude of "anything goes" dominated these schools. In one such school I visited, a troubled boy was allowed to sit crunched up in his cubby the whole morning.

But Freud never meant that play was to be the major preoccupation of children nor that repression was "bad." It was *too much* repression, rather than repression per se, that could result in neuroses. In contrast to Montessori who regarded all adaptation as social adaptation, Freud distinguished two modes, or poles, of adaptation.[5] One of these involves satisfying the individual's basic needs for food, water, sex, self-esteem, and so on. These needs, at least initially, are expressed in a special mode of thinking that Freud called the "primary process." Primary-process thinking gives rise to dreams, jokes, slips of the tongue, fantasy, and play. All of these modes of expression vent the individual's needs and desires, particularly those not approved by society.

The second mode of adaptation has to do with the outside world of physical laws and social interactions. Inasmuch as we are biological beings we have to adapt to our physical environment, and as social beings, we must adapt to our social environment. For this adaptation we have a different mode of thinking that Freud called the "secondary process." In contrast to the primary process, which operates by means of imaginative substitutions, transformations, and condensations, the secondary process is essentially rational—it is geared to deal with environments that are essentially rule regulated.

Accordingly, from a Freudian point of view, healthy adaptation requires a kind of equilibrium between the needs of the individual and the needs of society. Healthy people need to be able to look after themselves before they can look after others. In a sense, play is an expression of self-love because by means of it the individual looks after his or her own needs. But play is healthy self-love in that it enables the individual to work and thus serve others.

Freud's distinction between the two modes of adaptation and between work and play as representing two somewhat opposed modes of adaptation were seconded by Jean Piaget.[6] Like Freud, Piaget distinguished two different modes of adaptation, which he called "assimilation" and "accommodation" respectively. In some ways, Piaget's assimilation was like Freud's primary process in that it can transform reality in nonrational ways and is concerned with the satisfaction of personal needs. Likewise, Piaget's notion of accommodation in some ways parallels Freud's notion of the secondary process in that it too is concerned with the individual's adaptation to the external world. For Piaget, as for Freud, play involves a transformation of reality in the service of satisfying personal needs. Both play and work, the primary and secondary processes, and accommodation and assimilation are necessary for healthy adaptation.

Over the last ten years in America, the Montessori idea that play is the child's work has replaced the Freud/Piaget view that play and work are separate but complementary activities. Indeed, one might define the abuse of hurrying as the pressure on children to make social accommodations at the expense of personal assimilations. From this point of view, hurried children work much more than they play, and this is the reason that they are so stressed. One evidence of this new negative attitude toward children's play is the rapid growth of Montessori schools in the past decade—there are now thousands of Montessori classrooms and schools all around the country, and the number keeps growing. By and large this is a healthy development because Montessori teachers are often better trained in the art of teaching than most young people who graduate from teachers' colleges. But the prejudice against play still exists and may be one reason parents are attracted to Montessori schools over the more conventional "play" preschools.

The following example illustrates how the dictum "play is the child's work" gets translated into teaching practice: While observing in one of my favorite nursery schools, I watched a group of four- and five-year-olds playing with some plastic dinousaurs. "I am going to eat you up," said one boy, moving his menacing looking beast close to his neighbor's. "You will have to catch me first, I'm faster than you," said the other boy as he ducked his smaller animal behind a wall of blocks. At this moment the teacher came over and decided to capitalize upon the children's interest (the so-called teaching moment) and to instruct them in some size concepts with the aid of the dinousaurs. "Which one is larger?" she asked. But the boys, clearly sniffing a teaching situation, quickly ended their dinousaur play and went on to other projects.

For young children dinousaurs have a great deal of symbolic significance—they are big and powerful. Yet, reduced in size and power by being rendered in plastic they are quite manageable. They are also remote and safe because there is little danger of encountering one in the street. Dinousaurs, then, provide children with a symbolic and safe way of dealing with the giants in their world, namely, adults. Young children are constantly being told "no" or "don't do that" or "leave that alone" or "get away from there." Adults frustrate them at every turn but are too big to combat directly. So children fight back indirectly and dinousaurs are stand-ins for controlling the world of giants. When the teacher interfered and tried to transform personal adaptation into social adaptation—play into work—the children gave up the game because their interest in dinousaurs was personal, not social.

Certainly, children need to learn size comparisons and their spontaneous interests can be a cue to teaching topics. And children need to do more than play. At every turn they are learning social rules—how to behave in a restaurant, on a plane, at a friend's house, how to put clothes on, how to take them off, how to eat with utensils, how to wash behind the ears, how to wipe oneself with a towel. Children are also learning basic concepts about space, time, number, color, and so on.

All of this, and much more social learning—such as described in chapter six—is the real work of childhood. But children need to be given an opportunity for pure play as well as for work. If adults feel that each spontaneous interest of a child is an opportunity for a lesson, the child's opportunities for pure play are foreclosed. At all levels of development, whether at home or at school, children need the opportunity to play for play's sake. Whether play is the symbolic play of young children, the games with rules and collections of the school-age child, or the more complicated intellectual games of adolescence (like Dungeons and Dragons) children should be given the time and encouragement to engage in them.

Basically, play is nature's way of dealing with stress for children as well as adults. As parents, we can help by investing in toys and playthings that give the greatest scope to the child's imagination. Windup and battery-operated toys are amusing because they behave in unexpected ways, but they leave little possibility for personal expression. Money spent on such toys could well be saved and put toward a good set of blocks that give children leeway to create and that can be used for years. Other materials such as crayons, paints, clay, and chalk are all creative playthings because they allow for the child's personal expression. It is not necessary to ask children what they have created, for they probably have no conscious idea. Asking about the meaning of a child's production is like the teacher trying to turn children's play with dinousaurs into an adult-oriented lesson plan.

As concerned citizens, we need to assert the value of the arts in the schools. The overemphasis on the basics in contemporary education without a corresponding emphasis on personal expression through the arts hurries children by destroying the necessary balance between work and play. The need for workers to have modes of personal expression at work is just beginning to be realized and appreciated by American industry. Schools need to recognize that children also work better, learn better, and yes, grow better, if time spent in social adaptation—learning the basics—is alternated with time periods given over to avenues for self-expression. Far from being a luxury, time and money spent on the arts enhances learning and development by reducing the stress of hurrying and by giving children an aesthetic perspective to balance the workday one.

Finally, as media consumers, we need to reassert the value of true play, and fantasy. The real need is for creative writers who can produce quality material for children that challenges the imagination as well as entertains. It would be a mistake to dismiss the value of fantasy because of the poor quality of material on most children's television programs and in many children's books. Imaginative fantasy has redeeming personal value and may have important social learning fringe benefits as well. The media need to provide better fantasy, fantasy such as fairy tales, which help children to deal with the stress of life.

HOW TO LIVE ON TWENTY-FOUR HOURS A DAY

The title of this section is borrowed from a book by Arnold Bennett, novelist, playwright, and self-help specialist.[7] In the title he incorporated a time-honored strategy for dealing with stress that has been passed down by philosophers such as Epictetus and warriors such as Marcus Aurelius. Basically, their message is that much of human stress and misery comes from dwelling in the past, on what might have been, or in the future, on what will be. In fact, there is nothing to do about the past and the future is problematic. We only have control over the present, and this is where we need to direct our energies.

Unfortunately, this approach is sometimes misunderstood as an argument for hedonism. "Enjoy today for tomorrow you may die." But this was not the intent of the philosophers. They saw life as a whole, guided by moral purpose and principle. While each day was to be lived on its own terms, those terms had to be in accord with the abiding laws of society and ethics.

> *Every moment think steadily as a Roman and a man to do what thou hast in hand with perfect and simple dignity, and feeling of affection, and freedom and justice and to give thyself relief from all other thoughts. And thou wilt give thyself relief if thou doest every act of thy life as if it were thy last, laying aside all carelessness and passionate aversion from the commands of reason, and all hypocrisy and self love, and discontent with the portion which has been given to thee.*[8]

198

Although children are too young to appreciate these thoughts, they can learn from parental action. If we concentrate on the here and now, without worrying about yesterday or tomorrow, our children will do likewise. If you are a working mother, enjoy the time you spend with your child and don't spoil it for him or her by worrying about the time you were not around or about the times you will be separated in the future. Children live in the present, and they know when we are with them physically but not mentally. By worrying about the past and future, we lose the present and our children don't have us, even when we are around.

Over the years, I have made it a practice to take a little time for myself each day, to enjoy a sunset, watch a sparrow, admire a snowflake. Such moments can and should be shared with children. I also take a moment to review the events of the day, to evaluate, without regret, how well I lived up to the goals of devoting full energies to the task at hand. My sense is that such practices are communicated to the children we live with and that the more we incorporate stress relief valves into our daily routines, the more children can learn similar strategies.

I have outlined above one of many different philosophies or styles for the art of living. Hans Selye, for example, argues for "altruistic egotism"—in effect, that we serve ourselves by serving others. And Albert Schweitzer had a philosophy he called "Reverence for Life," according to which all living things were to be valued. No one philosophy of life will satisfy everyone, but everyone needs a philosophy of life, a way of seeing it whole and in perspective. The art of living is the most difficult task children have to learn, and they do this best if their parents or caretakers have a way of looking at life as a whole.

No matter what philosophy of life we espouse, it is important to see childhood as a stage of life, not just as the anteroom to life. Hurrying children into adulthood violates the sanctity of life by giving one period priority over another. But if we really value human life, we will value each period equally and give unto each stage of life what is appropriate to that stage.

A philosophy of life, an art of living, is essentially a way of decentering, a way of looking at our lives in perspective and of recognizing the needs and rights of others. If we can overcome some of the stresses of our adult lives and decenter, we can begin to appreciate the value of childhood with its own special joys, sorrows, worries, and rewards. Valuing childhood does not mean seeing it as a happy innocent period but, rather, as an important period of life to which children are entitled. It is children's right to be children, to enjoy the pleasures, and to suffer the pains of a childhood that is infringed by hurrying. In the end, a childhood is the most basic human right of children.

Notes

CHAPTER 1

1. J. J. Rousseau, *Emile.* New York: Dutton, 1957.
2. A. Toffler, *The Third Wave.* New York: Bantam, 1980.
3. Toffler, ibid.
4. A. B. Alcott, *Observations on the Principles and Methods of Infant Instruction.* Boston: Carter & Hendee, 1830.
5. M. W. Shinn, *The Biography of a Baby.* Boston, Houghton Mifflin, 1900; J. Piaget, *The Origins of Intelligence in the Child.* New York: International Universities Press, 1952.
6. E. L. Holt, *The Care and Feeding of Children.* New York: Appleton, 1903.
7. Arnold L. Gesell, *The Mental Growth of the Pre-School Child.* New York: Macmillan, 1968; Benjamin M. Spock, *Baby and Child Care.* New York: Dutton, 1976.
8. K. Olness, *Raising Happy, Healthy Children.* Wayzata, Minnesota: Meadowbrook Press, 1977; Roger W. McIntire, *For Love of Children.* Del Mar, California: CRM Books, 1970; G. Ron Norton, *Parenting.* Englewood Cliffs, N.J.: Prentice-Hall, 1977; Harold Russell and Thomas P. Kelly, Jr., *The Parent Book.* San Diego: Graphic Publishers, 1977; M. L. Bettinger (ed.), *Living With Your Hyperactive Child.* New York: BPS Books, Inc., 1977; Sydney B. Simon and Sally Wendkos Olds, *Helping Your Child Learn Right from Wrong.* New York: McGraw-Hill, 1977.
9. J. Bruner, *The Process of Education.* Cambridge, Massachusetts: Harvard University Press, 1960.
10. J. C. Holt, *How Children Fail.* New York: Pitman, 1964.
11. J. Kozol, *Death at an Early Age.* Boston: Houghton Mifflin, 1967.
12. H. R. Kohl, *36 Children.* New York: New American Library, 1967.
13. Arnold L. Gesell, Louise B. Ames, and Frances L. Ilg, *Infant and Child in the Culture of Today.* New York: Harper & Row, 1943.
14. S. Ferraro, "Hotsy Totsy," *American Way Magazine,* April, 1981, p. 61.
15. C. Emerson, "Summer Camp, It's Not the Same Anymore," *Sky,* March, 1981, 29–34.
16. J. Hatfield, "Going it alone? It's kids stuff," *The Boston Globe,* Sunday, June 7, 1981.
17. Patricia O'Brien, "Dope, Sex, Crime, What Happened to Childhood," *Chicago Tribune,* March 8, 1981.

18. "The Games Teen Agers Play," *Newsweek*, September 1, 1980.
19. Ibid.
20. E. M. Hetherington, M. Cos, and R. Cox, "The Aftermath of Divorce." In J. H. Stevens, Jr. & M. Mathews (Ed.s) *Mother-child, father-child relations*. Washington, D.C.: NAEYC, 1978.
21. Michael Coakley, "Robert, a Robber at Age 9, and Just One of Thousands," *Chicago Tribune*, March 8, 1981.
22. G. Getschow, and B. R. Schiener, "Family Portrait: Friends View Parents of Hinckley as Loving, Devoted to Children," *Wall Street Journal*, April 6, 1981.
23. E. H. Erikson, *Childhood and Society*. New York: Norton, 1950.
24. "Suicide Belt," *Time Magazine*. September 1, 1980.
25. Ibid.

CHAPTER 2

1. W. Whitman, *Leaves of Grass*. New York: New American Library, 1980.
2. J. Piaget, *The Psychology of Intelligence*. London: Routledge & Kegan Paul, 1950.
3. J. Locke, *An Essay Concerning Human Understanding*. New York: E. P. Dutton, 1961.
4. John Watson, *Psychological Care of Infant and Child*. New York: Norton, 1928.
5. B. F. Skinner, *Walden Two*. New York: Macmillan, 1948.
6. Tom Wolfe, "The 'Me Decade' and the Third Great Awakening," *New York*, 23 August, 1976, pp 26–40.
7. C. Lasch, *The Culture of Narcissism*. New York: Norton, 1979.
8. J. Underwood, "A Game Plan for America," *Sports Illustrated*, February 23, 1981.
9. Underwood, ibid.
10. Ibid.
11. Ibid.
12. Dora Phinney, "A Study of Parents Perceptions of the Effects of Delayed Kindergarten." M.A. Thesis, Dept. of Education, California State University, Northridge, 1979.
13. Colette Dowling, "The Cinderella Syndrome," *New York Times Magazine*, March 22, 1981.
14. K. M. Pierce, "Big Crunch for Kindergartens," *Time*, September 29, 1980.
15. Ibid.

CHAPTER 3

1. A. Binet, and H. Simon, "Methodes Nouvelles pour le Diagnostic du Nouveau Intellectual des Anormaux," *L'Année Psychologique* 1905, *11*, 245–236.
2. Ibid.
3. W. A. Shine, and N. Goldman, "Governance by Testing in New Jersey," *Educational Leadership*, December, 1980, pp 197–198.
4. Ibid.
5. F. G. Burke, "Testing in New Jersey," *Educational Leadership*, December 1980, 199–201.

6. J. O. Grambs, "Forty Years of Education: Can the Next Forty Be Any Better?" *Educational Leadership*, May 1981, p 651–655.

7. K. Keniston, "The 11-year olds of Today are the Computer Terminals of Tomorrow," *New York Times*, Feb. 19, 1976.

8. F. Niedermeyer, and S. Yelon, "Los Angeles Aligns Instruction with Essential Skills," *Educational Leadership*, May 1981, p 618.

9. Ibid.

10. H. M. Brickell, "How to Change What Matters," *Educational Leadership*, December, 1980, p 202–207.

11. W. J. Popham, and S. C. Rankin, "Detroit's Measurement Driven Instruction," *Educational Leadership*, December, 1980.

12. Jeffrey K. Smith, and M. Katims, "Reading in the City: the Chicago Mastery Learning Reading Program," *Phi Delta Kappan*, 1977, 59, 199–202.

13. Stanley G. Hall, *Adolescence: Its Psychology and its Relations to Pedagogy, Anthropology, Sociology, Sex, Crime, Religion and Education.* 2 vols. New York: D. Appleton, 1904.

14. C. Horner, "Is the New Sex Education Going Too Far?" *New York Times Magazine*, December 7, 1980 quote 138.

15. Ibid.

16. P. Buck, "Sex Education Belongs in the Schools," *Educational Leadership*, February 1981, p. 38, pp. 390–395.

17. Ibid.

18. Ibid.

19. B. Bettelheim, "Our Children are Treated like Idiots," *Psychology Today*, July, 1981, pp 28–44.

20. Ibid.

21. S. Engelmann, and T. Engelmann, *Give Your Child a Superior Mind.* New York: Cornerstone, 1981; E. Gregg, and J. Knotts, *Growing Wisdom, Growing Wonder.* New York: Macmillan, 1980; Joan Beck, *How to Raise a Brighter Child.* New York: Pocket Books, 1975; H. Simon, and S. Olds, *Helping your Child Learn Right from Wrong.* New York: McGraw-Hill, 1977; D. Butler, *Cushla and her Books.* Boston: Horn Book Inc., 1980; M. L. Bittinger (Ed.), *Living with Your Hyperactive Child.* New York: BPS Books Inc., 1977.

22. Gregg and Knotts, ibid.

23. Engelmann and Engelmann, ibid.

24. Engelmann and Engelmann, ibid.

25. Engelmann and Engelmann, ibid.

26. V. Goertzel, and M. G. Goertzel, *Cradles of Eminence.* Boston: Little Brown, 1962.

27. Ibid.

28. M. Deacon, *The Children on the Hill.* New York: Ballantine Books, 1975.

CHAPTER 4

1. M. McLuhan, *Understanding Media.* New York: Mentor, 1964.

2. E. Kaye, *The ACT Guide to Children's Television.* Boston: Beacon Press, 1979.

3. L. Kronenberger, *Uncivilized and Uncivilizing.* TV Guide, February 1966.

4. McLuhan, ibid.

5. Geoffrey Cowan, *See No Evil.* New York: Touchstone, 1980.

6. Ibid.

7. Ibid.

8. Kaye, ibid.

9. L. Loevinger, "There Need be No Apology, No Lament." *TV Guide*, April 1968.

10. G. Weinberg, "What is Television's World of the Single Parent Doing to Your Family," *TV Guide*, August, 1970.

11. Martin Mayer, "Out of Shape," *TV Guide*, July 1962.

12. McLuhan, ibid.

13. Marie Winn, "What Became of Childhood Innocence," *New York Times Magazine*, January 25, 1981.

14. Ibid.

15. B. Bettelheim, *The Uses of Enchantment.* New York: Vintage, 1977.

16. Ibid.

17. Winn, ibid.

18. Ibid.

19. Collette Dowling, *The Cinderella Complex.* New York: Summit, 1981.

20. Wilson Bryan Key, *Media Sexploitation.* New York: Signet, 1977.

21. Ibid.

22. Ibid.

23. Ibid.

24. Ibid.

CHAPTER 5

1. J. Piaget, *The Psychology of Intelligence.* London: Routledge & Kegan Paul, 1950.

2. H. T. Epstein, "Learning to learn: Matching Instruction to Cognitive Levels," *Principal,* May 1981, 60, 25–30.

3. E. H. Erikson, *Childhood and Society.* New York: Norton, 1950.

4. J. Piaget, *The Construction of Reality in the Child.* New York: Basic Books, 1954.

5. J. Bowlby, *Attachment and Loss:* Vol. 1 *Attachment.* London: Hogarth, 1971.

6. Erikson, ibid.

7. E. Gosse, *Father and Son: A Study of Two Temperaments.* London: Heinemann, 1909.

8. H. S. Sullivan, *The Interpersonal Theory of Psychiatry.* New York: Norton, 1953.

9. M. E. Seligman, *Helplessness.* San Francisco: W. H. Freeman, 1975.

10. B. Inhelder, and J. Piaget, *The Growth of Logical Thinking from Childhood to Adolescence.* New York: Basic Books, 1958.

11. Piaget, ibid.

12. M. Twain, *Adventures of Tom Sawyer.* New York: Dodd, 1979.

CHAPTER 6

1. C. Lasch, *Haven in a Heartless World.* New York: Basic Books, 1977.

2. Talcott Parsons, *Social Structure and Personality.* New York: Free Press of Glencoe, 1964.

3. R. D. Laing, *The Politics of the Family and Other Essays.* New York: Pantheon Books, 1971.
4. A. Bandura, *Social Learning Theory.* Englewood Cliffs, N.J.: Prentice Hall, 1977.
5. B. F. Skinner, *Science and Human Behavior.* New York: Macmillan, 1953.
6. J. Piaget, *The Moral Judgment of the Child.* Glencoe, Ill.: The Free Press, 1960.
7. S. Freud, *A General Introduction to Psychoanalysis.* New York: Liveright, 1935.
8. E. Goffman, *Asylums.* Garden City, New York: Anchor Books, 1961.

CHAPTER 7

1. S. Freud, *A General Introduction to Psychoanalysis.* New York: Liveright, 1935.
2. H. Selye, *The Stress of Life.* New York: McGraw Hill, 1978.
3. Ibid.
4. W. B. Cannon, *The Wisdom of the Body.* New York: W. W. Norton, 1932.
5. S. Adler, and M. Gosnell, "Stress, How it Can Hurt, " *Time* April 21, 1980.
6. B. Ehrenreich, "Is Success Dangerous to Your Health?" *Ms.*, May, 1979.
7. Ibid.
8. Ibid.
9. G. Bach, and P. Wyden, *The Intimate Enemy.* New York: Morrow, 1969.
10. J. Bowlby, *Maternal Care and Mental Health.* Geneva: World Health Organization, 1951.
11. J. Kirsch, "California Kids," *New West.* July 1981, pp 66–73.
12. J. Segal, "When Business Travel Makes you an Absent Parent," *Frequent Flyer*, January 1981, pp. 42–46.
13. David Owen, "I Spied on the Twelfth Grade," *Esquire*, March, 1981.
14. Willard McGure, "Teacher Burn Out," *Today's Education* 1979, November–December.
15. J. Ourth, "The School Factor," *The Principal*, September, 1980, p. 40.
16. Leslie Hart, "Classrooms Are Killing Learning," *The Principal*, 1981, May 5, pp. 8–11.
17. T. J. Cottle, "Adolescent Voices," *Psychology Today*, February, 1979, p. 43.
18. M. McLuhan, *Understanding Media.* New York: Mentor, 1964.
19. Toronto *Star*, Sept. 3, 1980.

CHAPTER 8

1. J. B. Kelly, and J. S. Wallenstein, "Children of Divorce," *The Principal*, October, 1979, pp 51–58.
2. Ibid.
3. A. Evans, and J. Neel, "School Behaviors of Children from One Parent and Two Parent Homes," *The Principal*, September 1980, p. 38–39.
4. K. Barrett, "I Always Knew You'd Find Me, Mom," *Ladies Home Journal*, August, 1981, pp. 86, 77, 151, 152.
5. P. Hluchy, "Depressed Can Find Help at Metro Centers," *Toronto Star*, March 7, 1981.

6. K. A. Matthews, "Efforts at Control by Children and Adults with Type A Coronary-Prone Behavior Pattern," *Child Development,* 1979, *50,* pp. 842–847.

7. "Study Says Heart Ills Can Begin in Childhood," *The New York Times,* March 19, 1981.

8. Karen A. Matthews, "Antecedents of the Type A Coronary-Prone Behavior Pattern." In S. S. Brehn, S. M. Kassen, F. X. Gibbons (Ed.s) *Developmental Social Psychology.* New York: Oxford, 1981, pp. 235–248.

9. R. L. Veniga, and J. P. Spradley, *The Work Stress Connection.* Boston: Little Brown, 1981.

10. Stephanie Sevick, "Students Driven to Succeed," *Hartford Courant,* July 13, 1981.

11. Ibid.

12. M. E. R. Seligman, *Helplessness.* San Francisco: W. H. Freeman, 1975.

13. Ibid.

14. Ibid.

15. Megan Marshall, "Musical Wonder Kids," *The Boston Globe Magazine,* July 25, 1981.

16. Ibid.

17. Ibid.

18. Lois B. Murphy, *Widening World of Childhood.* New York: Basic Books, 1962.

19. M. Pinas, "Superkids," *Psychology Today,* January, 1979, pp. 52–63.

CHAPTER 9

1. Janet Marks, "Crises Intervention for Children: A Psychological Stitch in Time," *Town & Country,* October, 1980.

2. Herbert Spencer, *Education: Intellectual, Moral, and Physical.* New York: A.L. Fowle, 1860.

3. K. Groos, *The Play of Man.* New York: Appleton, 1901.

4. M. Montessori, *The Absorbent Mind.* New York: Delta, 1967.

5. S. Freud, "Formulations Regarding the Two Principles of Mental Functioning," 1911. In *Standard Edition of Complete Works,* Vol. 7. London: Hogarth, 1958.

6. J. Piaget, *Play, Dreams and Imitation in Childhood.* New York: Norton, 1962.

7. A. Bennett, *How to Live on Twenty-four Hours a Day.* New York: Wm. H. Wise, 1905.

8. M. Aurelius, *Meditations.* Chicago: Henry Regency, 1949.

Index

Comic books, 80
Competitive sports, 9
"Concrete operations," 103, 104, 106, 107, 122
Conflict and emotional distress, 141
Contract Evaluation Form, 185
Contracting, 124, 185
Contractual violations and hurrying, 133–136, 184, 190
Coping with stress, 181–182
Cottle, Thomas, 158
Creative playthings, 197
Creative writers, 198
Crimes by children, 25
Cults, 17, 18, 117, 124, 132
"Culture of narcissism," 26
Curiosity, 102

Decision making, 40
Delinquent children, 179
Delinquents, 191
Democracy in education, 68
Democratic parents, 125
Depression, 168
Detroit, 54, 55
Developmental hurrying, 184
Distress reactions, 142
Divorce, 20, 21, 26, 41, 153, 166, 167
Divorce rate, 13
Divorces, 9
Dowling, Colette, 36
Drug and alcohol use, 172
Drugs, 115
Dual-career couples, 20
Dungeons and Dragons, 85

Early Mental Traits of Three Hundred Geniuses, 63
Egalitarian movement, 21, 22
Ehrenreich, Barbara, 148
"Electric Company," 35
Emotional illness, 141
Emotional overload, 150, 151
Energic hurrying, 184
Energy consumption, 145
Engelmann and Engelmann, 63
Epstein, Herman, 97
Equilibrium, 146
Environmental disaster, 27
Erikson, Erik, 17, 108, 110, 116
Exploitation by parents, 191
Extended family, 38
Externalization, 121

Factory management systems, 51
Fairy tales, 82, 83
Falling in love, 116

Family life, 119
Fantasy, 85, 113
Ferraro, Susan, 8
"Fight or flight," 144
FORTRAN, 73
"Free-floating anxiety," 165–168
Freedom-responsibility contract, 124–127, 132, 136
Freidan, Betty, 38
Freud, Sigmund, 20, 66, 87, 116, 121, 141, 116, 177, 194, 195

Garmezy, Dr. Norman, 180
Gessell, Arnold, 5, 7
Goffman, Erving, 136
Grambs, Jean Dresden, 52, 53
Groos, Karl, 193
Growing up fast, 17, 21
Growing up slow, 97–118
Growth stages, 118

Hall, G. Stanley, 5, 56
Hart, Leslie A., 156
Hartford *Courant,* 172
Headstart, 7
Hechinger, Fred, 51
Helping hurried children, 183–200
Hetherington, Professor Mavis, 13
High technology, 25
Hinckley, John Warnock Jr., 15–17
Holt, Emmet T., 5
Holt, John, 7
Home schooling, 61–69
Homogenization of experience, 75
Homogenization of television, 77
Horner, Constance, 58
"Hotsy Totsy," 8
Hurried children, 3–22
Hurrying, 3, 11, 19, 20, 28, 29, 32, 35, 40, 97
  adolescents, 190–191
  in the media, 71–93
  by parents, 23, 25
  as rejection, 184, 186, 189
  school-age children, 189–190
  by schools, 47–49
  society, 183
  young children, 186–188

Identification, 121, 122
"Imaginary audience," 112, 113
Impression management, 181
Independence, 181
Industrialization, 4
Industrialization of school, 47
Infancy, 97, 98–100
Infant and Child Care, 6